on a more serious n

OUR COPYRIGHT NOTE

PUSH POWER BOSS JOURNAL + PLANNER

PUBLISHER
TA MEDIA & PRODUCTIONS LLC
DALLAS, TX 75240
www.PUBLISHYOURBOOKTODAY.INFO
WWW.TAMEDIACO.COM

let's get started

WHAT'S INSIDE

01

Reflect on 2021 to celebrate your big accomplishments and learn from your challenges. Set new 2022 intentions with actionable worksheets that will guide you to create achievable plans in your business. Plan out your days, weeks, and entire year with organized planners that will help you stay focused on what really matters. Set financial goals to help you grow your abundance mindset in your business.

let's get started

WHAT'S INSIDE

02

- QUOTE PAGE NOTE TO SELF (FILL-IN)
- DAILY INTENTION PAGES
- GRATITUDE JOURNAL PAGE
- PAST YEAR REFLECTION JOURNAL PAGES
- LOOKING FORWARD JOURNAL PAGES
- BLANK JOURNAL PAGES
- GOAL SETTING PAGES
- MONTHLY, WEEKLY,
- DAILY PLANNER PAGES
- PROJECT PLANNER PAGE
- FINANCIAL PLANNER
- PAGES
- HOLIDAYS
- 12 MONTHLY CALENDAR PAGES
- FILL-IN CALENDAR PAGE

bio

Cheronda Hester CEO of Push Power Boss. Her goal is to empower women in the areas of self-esteem, self-worth, and self-growth. By providing knowledge, direction, self-awareness through books, workshops, seminars, programs, one on one counseling, and mentorship. Developing women to add value to their present and futuristic spheres of influence. She is a true believer of Proverbs 27:17 “Iron Sharpens Iron”!

TRUE SUCCESS IS FOUND IN SEEKING GOD WITH OUR WHOLE HEART, MIND, SOUL, AND STRENGTH!!!!

FEAR
HAS TWO
MEANINGS,
FORGET EVERYTHING
AND RUN,
OR
FACE EVERYTHING
AND RISE,
THE CHOICE IS YOURS.

speaker, life coach, credit specialist

CHERONDA L. HESTER

CONNECT ACROSS ALL
SOCIAL MEDIA PLATFORMS
JOIN OUR EMAIL LIST AT
WWW.PUSHPOWERBOSS.COM

#pushpowerboss

quote of the year

ALWAYS

BELIEVE IN THE

IMPOSSIBLE

Cheronda Hester

NOTE TO SELF

dear, ____________________

YOU HAVE COME SO FAR THIS YEAR. LOOK AT ALL YOU'VE ACCOMPLISHED ALREADY. NEXT YEAR YOU WILL LOOK BACK & SEE YOU WERE ____________ ALL ALONG. IN A YEAR YOU'LL BE ____________ & ____________. I'M SO VERY PROUD OF YOU.

love you always,

____

SIGN YOUR NAME HERE

monthly intentions

MONTH OF:

OPEN PROJECTS

affirmations

I AM

MONTHLY INTENTIONS

01:

02:

03:

04:

05:

06:

07:

weekly priorities

WEEK OF:

MONDAY

TUESDAY

WEDNESDAY

THURSDAY

FRIDAY

SAT / SUN

DAILY FOCUS
monday
tuesday
wednesday
thursday
friday
saturday
sunday

DECIDE
COMMIT
SUCCEED

today's intentions

TODAY'S DATE:

TODAY'S TOP 3 INTENTIONS
01:
02:
03:

let's do this

today's affirmations

I AM

DAILY WATER TRACKER

HABIT TRACKER							
	M	T	W	T	F	S	S
	M	T	W	T	F	S	S
	M	T	W	T	F	S	S

today's intentions

TODAY'S DATE:

CALLS / EMAILS

HABIT TRACKER

DEADLINES

TODAY I AM THANKFUL FOR
01:
02:
03:

today's to do

FAITH
WITHOUT
WORK IS
DEAD

gratitude reflection

GRATITUDE LIST:

01:

02:

03:

04:

05:

06:

07:

08:

09:

10:

11:

PEOPLE I'M THANKFUL FOR:

01:

02:

03:

04:

05:

favorite memories

past year reflections

WHAT MOTIVATED YOU?

YOUR BIGGEST STRUGGLE?

TOP 3 ACCOMPLISHMENTS MADE THIS YEAR
01:
02:
03:

3 LESSONS LEARNED
01:
02:
03:

3 THINGS YOU CREATED
01:
02:
03:

WHAT WILL YOU TAKE WITH YOU IN 2022 & WHAT WILL YOU LEAVE BEHIND?

MAKE THINGS HAPPEN

past year reflections

DESCRIBE YOUR PAST YEAR IN ONE WORD

BIGGEST WINS OF THE YEAR
01:
02:
03:

BIGGEST CHALLENGES
01:
02:
03:

LESSONS LEARNED FROM WINS

01:

02:

03:

FROM CHALLENGES

01:

02:

03:

PEOPLE WHO SUPPORTED YOU THIS YEAR:

when you are finished, be sure to let these people know what they mean to you

Leadership
is based
On Inspiration,
Not Domination.
On Cooperation,
Not Intimidation.

looking forward

BRAINSTORM 10 WORDS THAT YOU WANT TO EMBODY 2022

3 SMALL MANIFESTATIONS
01:
02:
03:

3 BIG MANIFESTATIONS
01:
02:
03:

4 WAYS YOU WILL PUSH PAST YOUR COMFORT ZONE THIS YEAR
01:
02:
03:
04:

PICK ONE WORD FROM ABOVE TO EMBODY 2022

your abundance
is in
your faith

abundance journal

5 WORDS THAT DESCRIBE CURRENT BELIEFS TOWARDS MONEY

MONEY MANIFESTATIONS
01:
02:
03:
04:
05:
06:
07:

NEW OPPORTUNITIES TO MANIFEST MORE ABUNDANCE

MY ABUNDANCE MINDSET ALLOWS ME TO...

CURRENT RELATIONSHIP TO ABUNDANCE IN MY BUSINESS

ABUNDANCE AFFIRMATIONS
I AM

BRILLIANT *thoughts*

BRILLIANT *thoughts*

BRILLIANT *thoughts*

IF **YOU** CAN'T
STOP **THINKING**
ABOUT IT,
DON'T **STOP**
WORKING
FOR **IT.**

BRILLIANT *thoughts*

BRILLIANT *thoughts*

BRILLIANT *thoughts*

BRILLIANT *thoughts*

BRILLIANT *thoughts*

BRILLIANT *thoughts*

PUSH
THROUGH

BRILLIANT *thoughts*

BRILLIANT *thoughts*

BRILLIANT *thoughts*

BRILLIANT *thoughts*

BRILLIANT *thoughts*

BRILLIANT *thoughts*

BRILLIANT *thoughts*

BRILLIANT *thoughts*

Acting on even
a Twig of faith
Allows God to
to grow it.

BRILLIANT *thoughts*

BRILLIANT *thoughts*

BRILLIANT *thoughts*

WEEKLY GOALS *week of*

MONDAY GOAL

ACTIONS STEPS

TUESDAY GOAL

ACTIONS STEPS

WEDNESDAY GOAL

ACTIONS STEPS

THURSDAY GOAL

ACTIONS STEPS

FRIDAY GOAL

ACTIONS STEPS

SAT/SUN GOAL

ACTIONS STEPS

"

WHEN YOU'RE OVERWHELMED REMEMBER WHY YOU ARE DOING IT

this year's intentions

WORD OF THE YEAR:

BUSINESS INTENTIONS:

ACTION STEPS:

01

02

03

04

FINANCIAL INTENTIONS:

ACTION STEPS:

01

02

03

04

GROWTH INTENTIONS:

ACTION STEPS:

01

02

03

04

BUSINESS GOALS *today's date:*

NEW PROJECTS:

NEW CLIENTS:

FINANCIAL:

SOCIAL MEDIA:

MARKETING:

MINDSET:

I AM OPEN TO THE BEST THINGS IN LIFE

goal setting planner

START DATE: ______________________ DEADLINE: ______________________

MY BRILLIANT GOAL:

MY BIG WHY BEHIND THIS:

GOAL ACTION STEPS:	DEADLINE:
01:	
02:	
03:	
04:	
05:	
06:	
07:	
08:	
09:	

goal setting planner

START DATE: ______________________ DEADLINE: ______________________

MY BRILLIANT GOAL:

MY BIG WHY BEHIND THIS:

GOAL ACTION STEPS:	DEADLINE:
01:	
02:	
03:	
04:	
05:	
06:	
07:	
08:	
09:	

THE BEST
THING IS
**TO
BELIEVE
IN**
YOURSELF

DAY PLANNER *today's date:*

7:00
8:00
9:00
10:00
11:00
12:00
1:00
2:00
3:00
4:00
5:00
6:00
7:00
8:00

WEEKLY PLANNER

	morning	*afternoon*	*evening*
MON			
TUE			
WED			
THU			
FRI			
SAT			
SUN			

WIFE

MOM

BOSS

YEARLY PLANNER

write out your goals, intentions & plans

JAN

FEB

MAR

APR

MAY

JUN

JUL

AUG

SEP

OCT

NOV

DEC

PROJECT PLANNER

name of project:

	MON	TUE	WED	THU	FRI	SAT	SUN
WEEK 1							
WEEK 2							
WEEK 3							
WEEK 4							

PROJECT PLANNER *name of project:*

	MON	TUE	WED	THU	FRI	SAT	SUN
WEEK 1							
WEEK 2							
WEEK 3							
WEEK 4							

GO
WHERE
YOU *Feel*
MOST
alive

PROJECT PLANNER

name of project:

	MON	TUE	WED	THU	FRI	SAT	SUN
WEEK 1							
WEEK 2							
WEEK 3							
WEEK 4							

PROJECT PLANNER *name of project:*

	MON	TUE	WED	THU	FRI	SAT	SUN
WEEK 1							
WEEK 2							
WEEK 3							
WEEK 4							

PROJECT PLANNER

name of project:

	MON	TUE	WED	THU	FRI	SAT	SUN
WEEK 1							
WEEK 2							
WEEK 3							
WEEK 4							

PROJECT PLANNER *name of project:*

	MON	TUE	WED	THU	FRI	SAT	SUN
WEEK 1							
WEEK 2							
WEEK 3							
WEEK 4							

SALE GOALS & PROJECTIONS *month of:*

REVENUE GOAL:	
# OF SALES NEEDED:	

PRODUCT SOLD	QTY	AMOUNT

SALE LOCATION (ETSY, WEBSITE)	SALES TOTAL

FINAL INCOME:	
FINAL # OF SALES:	

INCOME & EXPENSES *yearly overview*

MONTH	EXPENSES	INCOME	TOTAL
JAN			
FEB			
MAR			
APR			
MAY			
JUN			
JUL			
AUG			
SEP			
OCT			
NOV			
DEC			

TOTAL NET INCOME: ____________________

INCOME & EXPENSES *monthly breakdown*

INCOME GOAL:	
SAVINGS GOAL:	

GROSS MONTHLY INCOME	AMOUNT

BILLS & EXPENSES	AMOUNT	DUE

TOTAL INCOME	
TOTAL EXPENSES	
TOTAL PROFIT/LOSS	

HOLIDAYS & DAYS OFF *rest and recharge*

JAN 01 NEW YEARS DAY	FEB 15 PRESIDENT'S DAY	MAY 10 MOTHER'S DAY
SEP 06 LABOR DAY	JUNE 20 FATHER'S DAY	NOV 11 VETERN'S DAY
NOV 25 THANKSGIVING	JUL 04 INDEPENDENCE DAY	DEC 24 CHRISTMAS EVE
DEC 25 CHRISTMAS DAY	MAY 31 MEMORIAL DAY	MAR 23 BIRTHDAY

2022
MONTHLY
CALENDAR

JANUARY

MONDAY	TUESDAY	WEDNESDAY	THURSDAY
3	4	5	6
10	11	12	13
17	18	19	20
24	25	26	27
31			

Notes

2022

TO DO

FRIDAY	SATURDAY	SUNDAY
	1	2
7	8	9
14	15	16
21	22	23
28	29	30

December

M	T	W	T	F	S	S
		1	2	3	4	5
6	7	8	9	10	11	12
13	14	15	16	17	18	19
20	21	22	23	24	25	26
27	28	29	30	31		

February

M	T	W	T	F	S	S
	1	2	3	4	5	6
7	8	9	10	11	12	13
14	15	16	17	18	19	20
21	22	23	24	25	26	27
28						

FEBRUARY

MONDAY	TUESDAY	WEDNESDAY	THURSDAY
	1	2	3
7	8	9	10
14	15	16	17
21	22	23	24
28			

Notes

2022

FRIDAY	SATURDAY	SUNDAY	TO DO
4	5	6	
11	12	13	
18	19	20	
25	26	27	

January

M	T	W	T	F	S	S
					1	2
3	4	5	6	7	8	9
10	11	12	13	14	15	16
17	18	19	20	21	22	23
24	25	26	27	28	29	30
31						

March

M	T	W	T	F	S	S
	1	2	3	4	5	6
7	8	9	10	11	12	13
14	15	16	17	18	19	20
21	22	23	24	25	26	27
28	29	30	31			

MARCH

MONDAY	TUESDAY	WEDNESDAY	THURSDAY
	1	2	3
7	8	9	10
14	15	16	17
21	22	23	24
28	29	30	31

Notes

2022

FRIDAY	SATURDAY	SUNDAY	TO DO
4	5	6	
11	12	13	
18	19	20	
25	26	27	

February

M	T	W	T	F	S	S
	1	2	3	4	5	6
7	8	9	10	11	12	13
14	15	16	17	18	19	20
21	22	23	24	25	26	27
28						

April

M	T	W	T	F	S	S
				1	2	3
4	5	6	7	8	9	10
11	12	13	14	15	16	17
18	19	20	21	22	23	24
25	26	27	28	29	30	

APRIL

MONDAY	TUESDAY	WEDNESDAY	THURSDAY
4	5	6	7
11	12	13	14
18	19	20	21
25	26	27	28

Notes

2022

TO DO

FRIDAY	SATURDAY	SUNDAY
1	2	3
8	9	10
15	16	17
22	23	24
29	30	

March

M	T	W	T	F	S	S
	1	2	3	4	5	6
7	8	9	10	11	12	13
14	15	16	17	18	19	20
21	22	23	24	25	26	27
28	29	30	31			

May

M	T	W	T	F	S	S
						1
2	3	4	5	6	7	8
9	10	11	12	13	14	15
16	17	18	19	20	21	22
23	24	25	26	27	28	29
30	31					

MAY

MONDAY	TUESDAY	WEDNESDAY	THURSDAY
2	3	4	5
9	10	11	12
16	17	18	19
23	24	25	26
30	31	**Notes**	

2022

TO DO

FRIDAY	SATURDAY	SUNDAY
		1
6	7	8
13	14	15
20	21	22
27	28	29

April

M	T	W	T	F	S	S
				1	2	3
4	5	6	7	8	9	10
11	12	13	14	15	16	17
18	19	20	21	22	23	24
25	26	27	28	29	30	

June

M	T	W	T	F	S	S
		1	2	3	4	5
6	7	8	9	10	11	12
13	14	15	16	17	18	19
20	21	22	23	24	25	26
27	28	29	30			

JUNE

MONDAY	TUESDAY	WEDNESDAY	THURSDAY
		1	2
6	7	8	9
13	14	15	16
20	21	22	23
27	28	29	30

Notes

2022

TO DO

FRIDAY	SATURDAY	SUNDAY
3	4	5
10	11	12
17	18	19
24	25	26

May

M	T	W	T	F	S	S
						1
2	3	4	5	6	7	8
9	10	11	12	13	14	15
16	17	18	19	20	21	22
23	24	25	26	27	28	29
30	31					

July

M	T	W	T	F	S	S
				1	2	3
4	5	6	7	8	9	10
11	12	13	14	15	16	17
18	19	20	21	22	23	24
25	26	27	28	29	30	31

JULY

MONDAY	TUESDAY	WEDNESDAY	THURSDAY
4	5	6	7
11	12	13	14
18	19	20	21
25	26	27	28

Notes

2022

TO DO

FRIDAY	SATURDAY	SUNDAY
1	2	3
8	9	10
15	16	17
22	23	24
29	30	31

June

M	T	W	T	F	S	S
		1	2	3	4	5
6	7	8	9	10	11	12
13	14	15	16	17	18	19
20	21	22	23	24	25	26
27	28	29	30			

August

M	T	W	T	F	S	S
1	2	3	4	5	6	7
8	9	10	11	12	13	14
15	16	17	18	19	20	21
22	23	24	25	26	27	28
29	30	31				

AUGUST

MONDAY	TUESDAY	WEDNESDAY	THURSDAY
1	2	3	4
8	9	10	11
15	16	17	18
22	23	24	25
29	30	31	

Notes

2022

TO DO

FRIDAY	SATURDAY	SUNDAY
5	6	7
12	13	14
19	20	21
26	27	28

July

M	T	W	T	F	S	S
				1	2	3
4	5	6	7	8	9	10
11	12	13	14	15	16	17
18	19	20	21	22	23	24
25	26	27	28	29	30	31

September

M	T	W	T	F	S	S
			1	2	3	4
5	6	7	8	9	10	11
12	13	14	15	16	17	18
19	20	21	22	23	24	25
26	27	28	29	30		

SEPTEMBER

MONDAY	TUESDAY	WEDNESDAY	THURSDAY
			1
5	6	7	8
12	13	14	15
19	20	21	22
26	27	28	29

Notes

2022

FRIDAY	SATURDAY	SUNDAY	TO DO
2	3	4	
9	10	11	
16	17	18	
23	24	25	
30			

August

M	T	W	T	F	S	S
1	2	3	4	5	6	7
8	9	10	11	12	13	14
15	16	17	18	19	20	21
22	23	24	25	26	27	28
29	30	31				

October

M	T	W	T	F	S	S
					1	2
3	4	5	6	7	8	9
10	11	12	13	14	15	16
17	18	19	20	21	22	23
24	25	26	27	28	29	30
31						

OCTOBER

MONDAY	TUESDAY	WEDNESDAY	THURSDAY
3	4	5	6
10	11	12	13
17	18	19	20
24	25	26	27
31	**Notes**		

2022

TO DO

FRIDAY	SATURDAY	SUNDAY
	1	2
7	8	9
14	15	16
21	22	23
28	29	30

September

M	T	W	T	F	S	S
			1	2	3	4
5	6	7	8	9	10	11
12	13	14	15	16	17	18
19	20	21	22	23	24	25
26	27	28	29	30		

November

M	T	W	T	F	S	S
	1	2	3	4	5	6
7	8	9	10	11	12	13
14	15	16	17	18	19	20
21	22	23	24	25	26	27
28	29	30				

NOVEMBER

MONDAY	TUESDAY	WEDNESDAY	THURSDAY
	1	2	3
7	8	9	10
14	15	16	17
21	22	23	24
28	29	30	

Notes

2022

FRIDAY	SATURDAY	SUNDAY	TO DO
4	5	6	
11	12	13	
18	19	20	
25	26	27	

October

M	T	W	T	F	S	S
					1	2
3	4	5	6	7	8	9
10	11	12	13	14	15	16
17	18	19	20	21	22	23
24	25	26	27	28	29	30
31						

December

M	T	W	T	F	S	S
			1	2	3	4
5	6	7	8	9	10	11
12	13	14	15	16	17	18
19	20	21	22	23	24	25
26	27	28	29	30	31	

DECEMBER

MONDAY	TUESDAY	WEDNESDAY	THURSDAY
			1
5	6	7	8
12	13	14	15
19	20	21	22
26	27	28	29

Notes

FRIDAY	SATURDAY	SUNDAY	TO DO
2	3	4	
9	10	11	
16	17	18	
23	24	25	
30	31		

November

M	T	W	T	F	S	S
	1	2	3	4	5	6
7	8	9	10	11	12	13
14	15	16	17	18	19	20
21	22	23	24	25	26	27
28	29	30				

January

M	T	W	T	F	S	S
						1
2	3	4	5	6	7	8
9	10	11	12	13	14	15
16	17	18	19	20	21	22
23	24	25	26	27	28	29
30	31					

2022

DAILY PLANNER

2022

CALENDAR

JANUARY

MO	TU	WE	TH	FR	SA	SU
					1	2
3	4	5	6	7	8	9
10	11	12	13	14	15	16
17	18	19	20	21	22	23
24	25	26	27	28	29	30
31						

FEBRUARY

MO	TU	WE	TH	FR	SA	SU
	1	2	3	4	5	6
7	8	9	10	11	12	13
14	15	16	17	18	19	20
21	22	23	24	25	26	27
28						

MARCH

MO	TU	WE	TH	FR	SA	SU
	1	2	3	4	5	6
7	8	9	10	11	12	13
14	15	16	17	18	19	20
21	22	23	24	25	26	27
28	29	30	31			

APRIL

MO	TU	WE	TH	FR	SA	SU
				1	2	3
4	5	6	7	8	9	10
11	12	13	14	15	16	17
18	19	20	21	22	23	24
25	26	27	28	29	30	

MAY

MO	TU	WE	TH	FR	SA	SU
						1
2	3	4	5	6	7	8
9	10	11	12	13	14	15
16	17	18	19	20	21	22
23	24	25	26	27	28	29
30	31					

JUNE

MO	TU	WE	TH	FR	SA	SU
		1	2	3	4	5
6	7	8	9	10	11	12
13	14	15	16	17	18	19
20	21	22	23	24	25	26
27	28	29	30			

JULY

MO	TU	WE	TH	FR	SA	SU
				1	2	3
4	5	6	7	8	9	10
11	12	13	14	15	16	17
18	19	20	21	22	23	24
25	26	27	28	29	30	31

AUGUST

MO	TU	WE	TH	FR	SA	SU
1	2	3	4	5	6	7
8	9	10	11	12	13	14
15	16	17	18	19	20	21
22	23	24	25	26	27	28
29	30	31				

SEPTEMBER

MO	TU	WE	TH	FR	SA	SU
			1	2	3	4
5	6	7	8	9	10	11
12	13	14	15	16	17	18
19	20	21	22	23	24	25
26	27	28	29	30		

OCTOBER

MO	TU	WE	TH	FR	SA	SU
					1	2
3	4	5	6	7	8	9
10	11	12	13	14	15	16
17	18	19	20	21	22	23
24	25	26	27	28	29	30
31						

NOVEMBER

MO	TU	WE	TH	FR	SA	SU
	1	2	3	4	5	6
7	8	9	10	11	12	13
14	15	16	17	18	19	20
21	22	23	24	25	26	27
28	29	30				

DECEMBER

MO	TU	WE	TH	FR	SA	SU
			1	2	3	4
5	6	7	8	9	10	11
12	13	14	15	16	17	18
19	20	21	22	23	24	25
26	27	28	29	30	31	

DAILY PLANNER

TODAY IS /

WEATHER

TODAY I AM EXCITED ABOUT

TODAY I AM GRATEFUL FOR

TODAY'S TOP PRIORITY

1.

2.

3.

TO DO LIST

TODAY'S SCHEDULE

PLAN		TRACK
	5.AM	
	6.AM	
	7.AM	
	8.AM	
	9.AM	
	10.AM	
	11.AM	
	12.PM	
	1.PM	
	3.PM	
	4.PM	
	5.PM	
	6.PM	
	7.PM	
	8.PM	
	9.PM	
	10.PM	
	11.PM	
	12.AM	

BREAKFAST

LUNCH

DINNER

WATER

HAPPY SCALE

MY REWARD

DAILY PLANNER

TODAY IS /

WEATHER

TODAY I AM EXCITED ABOUT

TODAY I AM GRATEFUL FOR

TODAY'S TOP PRIORITY

1.

2.

3.

TO DO LIST

TODAY'S SCHEDULE

PLAN		TRACK
	5.AM	
	6.AM	
	7.AM	
	8.AM	
	9.AM	
	10.AM	
	11.AM	
	12.PM	
	1.PM	
	3.PM	
	4.PM	
	5.PM	
	6.PM	
	7.PM	
	8.PM	
	9.PM	
	10.PM	
	11.PM	
	12.AM	

BREAKFAST

LUNCH

DINNER

WATER

HAPPY SCALE

MY REWARD

DAILY PLANNER

TODAY IS /

WEATHER

TODAY I AM EXCITED ABOUT

TODAY I AM GRATEFUL FOR

TODAY'S TOP PRIORITY

1.

2.

3.

TO DO LIST

TODAY'S SCHEDULE

PLAN		TRACK
	5.AM	
	6.AM	
	7.AM	
	8.AM	
	9.AM	
	10.AM	
	11.AM	
	12.PM	
	1.PM	
	3.PM	
	4.PM	
	5.PM	
	6.PM	
	7.PM	
	8.PM	
	9.PM	
	10.PM	
	11.PM	
	12.AM	

BREAKFAST

LUNCH

DINNER

WATER

HAPPY SCALE

MY REWARD

DAILY PLANNER

TODAY IS /

WEATHER

TODAY I AM EXCITED ABOUT

TODAY I AM GRATEFUL FOR

TODAY'S TOP PRIORITY

1.
2.
3.

TO DO LIST

TODAY'S SCHEDULE

PLAN		TRACK
	5.AM	
	6.AM	
	7.AM	
	8.AM	
	9.AM	
	10.AM	
	11.AM	
	12.PM	
	1.PM	
	3.PM	
	4.PM	
	5.PM	
	6.PM	
	7.PM	
	8.PM	
	9.PM	
	10.PM	
	11.PM	
	12.AM	

BREAKFAST

LUNCH

DINNER

WATER

HAPPY SCALE

MY REWARD

DAILY PLANNER

TODAY IS /

WEATHER

TODAY I AM EXCITED ABOUT

TODAY I AM GRATEFUL FOR

TODAY'S TOP PRIORITY

1.

2.

3.

TO DO LIST

TODAY'S SCHEDULE

PLAN		TRACK
	5.AM	
	6.AM	
	7.AM	
	8.AM	
	9.AM	
	10.AM	
	11.AM	
	12.PM	
	1.PM	
	3.PM	
	4.PM	
	5.PM	
	6.PM	
	7.PM	
	8.PM	
	9.PM	
	10.PM	
	11.PM	
	12.AM	

BREAKFAST

LUNCH

DINNER

WATER

HAPPY SCALE

MY REWARD

DAILY PLANNER

TODAY IS /

WEATHER

TODAY I AM EXCITED ABOUT

TODAY I AM GRATEFUL FOR

TODAY'S TOP PRIORITY

1.

2.

3.

TO DO LIST

TODAY'S SCHEDULE

PLAN		TRACK
	5.AM	
	6.AM	
	7.AM	
	8.AM	
	9.AM	
	10.AM	
	11.AM	
	12.PM	
	1.PM	
	3.PM	
	4.PM	
	5.PM	
	6.PM	
	7.PM	
	8.PM	
	9.PM	
	10.PM	
	11.PM	
	12.AM	

BREAKFAST

LUNCH

DINNER

WATER

HAPPY SCALE

MY REWARD

DAILY PLANNER

TODAY IS /

WEATHER

TODAY I AM EXCITED ABOUT

TODAY I AM GRATEFUL FOR

TODAY'S TOP PRIORITY

1.

2.

3.

TO DO LIST

TODAY'S SCHEDULE

PLAN		TRACK
	5.AM	
	6.AM	
	7.AM	
	8.AM	
	9.AM	
	10.AM	
	11.AM	
	12.PM	
	1.PM	
	3.PM	
	4.PM	
	5.PM	
	6.PM	
	7.PM	
	8.PM	
	9.PM	
	10.PM	
	11.PM	
	12.AM	

BREAKFAST

LUNCH

DINNER

WATER

HAPPY SCALE

MY REWARD

DAILY PLANNER

TODAY IS /

WEATHER

TODAY I AM EXCITED ABOUT

TODAY I AM GRATEFUL FOR

TODAY'S TOP PRIORITY

1.

2.

3.

TO DO LIST

TODAY'S SCHEDULE

PLAN		TRACK
	5.AM	
	6.AM	
	7.AM	
	8.AM	
	9.AM	
	10.AM	
	11.AM	
	12.PM	
	1.PM	
	3.PM	
	4.PM	
	5.PM	
	6.PM	
	7.PM	
	8.PM	
	9.PM	
	10.PM	
	11.PM	
	12.AM	

BREAKFAST

LUNCH

DINNER

WATER

HAPPY SCALE

MY REWARD

DAILY PLANNER

TODAY IS /

WEATHER

TODAY I AM EXCITED ABOUT

TODAY I AM GRATEFUL FOR

TODAY'S TOP PRIORITY

1.

2.

3.

TO DO LIST

TODAY'S SCHEDULE

PLAN		TRACK
	5.AM	
	6.AM	
	7.AM	
	8.AM	
	9.AM	
	10.AM	
	11.AM	
	12.PM	
	1.PM	
	3.PM	
	4.PM	
	5.PM	
	6.PM	
	7.PM	
	8.PM	
	9.PM	
	10.PM	
	11.PM	
	12.AM	

BREAKFAST

LUNCH

DINNER

WATER

HAPPY SCALE

MY REWARD

DAILY PLANNER

TODAY IS /

WEATHER

TODAY I AM EXCITED ABOUT

TODAY I AM GRATEFUL FOR

TODAY'S TOP PRIORITY

1.

2.

3.

TO DO LIST

TODAY'S SCHEDULE

PLAN		TRACK
	5.AM	
	6.AM	
	7.AM	
	8.AM	
	9.AM	
	10.AM	
	11.AM	
	12.PM	
	1.PM	
	3.PM	
	4.PM	
	5.PM	
	6.PM	
	7.PM	
	8.PM	
	9.PM	
	10.PM	
	11.PM	
	12.AM	

BREAKFAST

LUNCH

DINNER

WATER

HAPPY SCALE

MY REWARD

DAILY PLANNER

TODAY IS /

WEATHER

TODAY I AM EXCITED ABOUT

TODAY I AM GRATEFUL FOR

TODAY'S TOP PRIORITY

1.

2.

3.

TO DO LIST

TODAY'S SCHEDULE

PLAN		TRACK
	5.AM	
	6.AM	
	7.AM	
	8.AM	
	9.AM	
	10.AM	
	11.AM	
	12.PM	
	1.PM	
	3.PM	
	4.PM	
	5.PM	
	6.PM	
	7.PM	
	8.PM	
	9.PM	
	10.PM	
	11.PM	
	12.AM	

BREAKFAST

LUNCH

DINNER

WATER

HAPPY SCALE

MY REWARD

DAILY PLANNER

TODAY IS /

WEATHER

TODAY I AM EXCITED ABOUT

TODAY I AM GRATEFUL FOR

TODAY'S TOP PRIORITY

1.

2.

3.

TO DO LIST

TODAY'S SCHEDULE

PLAN		TRACK
	5.AM	
	6.AM	
	7.AM	
	8.AM	
	9.AM	
	10.AM	
	11.AM	
	12.PM	
	1.PM	
	3.PM	
	4.PM	
	5.PM	
	6.PM	
	7.PM	
	8.PM	
	9.PM	
	10.PM	
	11.PM	
	12.AM	

BREAKFAST

LUNCH

DINNER

WATER

HAPPY SCALE

MY REWARD

DAILY PLANNER

TODAY IS /

WEATHER

TODAY I AM EXCITED ABOUT

TODAY I AM GRATEFUL FOR

TODAY'S TOP PRIORITY

1.

2.

3.

TO DO LIST

TODAY'S SCHEDULE

PLAN		TRACK
	5.AM	
	6.AM	
	7.AM	
	8.AM	
	9.AM	
	10.AM	
	11.AM	
	12.PM	
	1.PM	
	3.PM	
	4.PM	
	5.PM	
	6.PM	
	7.PM	
	8.PM	
	9.PM	
	10.PM	
	11.PM	
	12.AM	

BREAKFAST

LUNCH

DINNER

WATER

HAPPY SCALE

MY REWARD

DAILY PLANNER

TODAY IS /

WEATHER

TODAY I AM EXCITED ABOUT

TODAY I AM GRATEFUL FOR

TODAY'S TOP PRIORITY

1.

2.

3.

TO DO LIST

TODAY'S SCHEDULE

PLAN		TRACK
	5.AM	
	6.AM	
	7.AM	
	8.AM	
	9.AM	
	10.AM	
	11.AM	
	12.PM	
	1.PM	
	3.PM	
	4.PM	
	5.PM	
	6.PM	
	7.PM	
	8.PM	
	9.PM	
	10.PM	
	11.PM	
	12.AM	

BREAKFAST

LUNCH

DINNER

WATER

HAPPY SCALE

MY REWARD

DAILY PLANNER

TODAY IS /

WEATHER

TODAY I AM EXCITED ABOUT

TODAY I AM GRATEFUL FOR

TODAY'S TOP PRIORITY

1.

2.

3.

TO DO LIST

TODAY'S SCHEDULE

PLAN		TRACK
	5.AM	
	6.AM	
	7.AM	
	8.AM	
	9.AM	
	10.AM	
	11.AM	
	12.PM	
	1.PM	
	3.PM	
	4.PM	
	5.PM	
	6.PM	
	7.PM	
	8.PM	
	9.PM	
	10.PM	
	11.PM	
	12.AM	

BREAKFAST

LUNCH

DINNER

WATER

HAPPY SCALE

MY REWARD

DAILY PLANNER

TODAY IS /

WEATHER

TODAY I AM EXCITED ABOUT

TODAY I AM GRATEFUL FOR

TODAY'S TOP PRIORITY

1.
2.
3.

TO DO LIST

TODAY'S SCHEDULE

PLAN		TRACK
	5.AM	
	6.AM	
	7.AM	
	8.AM	
	9.AM	
	10.AM	
	11.AM	
	12.PM	
	1.PM	
	3.PM	
	4.PM	
	5.PM	
	6.PM	
	7.PM	
	8.PM	
	9.PM	
	10.PM	
	11.PM	
	12.AM	

BREAKFAST

LUNCH

DINNER

WATER

HAPPY SCALE

MY REWARD

DAILY PLANNER

TODAY IS /

WEATHER

TODAY I AM EXCITED ABOUT

TODAY I AM GRATEFUL FOR

TODAY'S TOP PRIORITY

1.

2.

3.

TO DO LIST

TODAY'S SCHEDULE

PLAN		TRACK
	5.AM	
	6.AM	
	7.AM	
	8.AM	
	9.AM	
	10.AM	
	11.AM	
	12.PM	
	1.PM	
	3.PM	
	4.PM	
	5.PM	
	6.PM	
	7.PM	
	8.PM	
	9.PM	
	10.PM	
	11.PM	
	12.AM	

BREAKFAST

LUNCH

DINNER

WATER

HAPPY SCALE

MY REWARD

DAILY PLANNER

TODAY IS /

WEATHER

TODAY I AM EXCITED ABOUT

TODAY I AM GRATEFUL FOR

TODAY'S TOP PRIORITY

1.

2.

3.

TO DO LIST

TODAY'S SCHEDULE

PLAN		TRACK
	5.AM	
	6.AM	
	7.AM	
	8.AM	
	9.AM	
	10.AM	
	11.AM	
	12.PM	
	1.PM	
	3.PM	
	4.PM	
	5.PM	
	6.PM	
	7.PM	
	8.PM	
	9.PM	
	10.PM	
	11.PM	
	12.AM	

BREAKFAST

LUNCH

DINNER

WATER

HAPPY SCALE

MY REWARD

DAILY PLANNER

TODAY IS /

WEATHER

TODAY I AM EXCITED ABOUT

TODAY I AM GRATEFUL FOR

TODAY'S TOP PRIORITY

1.

2.

3.

TO DO LIST

TODAY'S SCHEDULE

PLAN		TRACK
	5.AM	
	6.AM	
	7.AM	
	8.AM	
	9.AM	
	10.AM	
	11.AM	
	12.PM	
	1.PM	
	3.PM	
	4.PM	
	5.PM	
	6.PM	
	7.PM	
	8.PM	
	9.PM	
	10.PM	
	11.PM	
	12.AM	

BREAKFAST

LUNCH

DINNER

WATER

HAPPY SCALE

MY REWARD

DAILY PLANNER

TODAY IS /

WEATHER

TODAY I AM EXCITED ABOUT

TODAY I AM GRATEFUL FOR

TODAY'S TOP PRIORITY

1.

2.

3.

TO DO LIST

TODAY'S SCHEDULE

PLAN		TRACK
	5.AM	
	6.AM	
	7.AM	
	8.AM	
	9.AM	
	10.AM	
	11.AM	
	12.PM	
	1.PM	
	3.PM	
	4.PM	
	5.PM	
	6.PM	
	7.PM	
	8.PM	
	9.PM	
	10.PM	
	11.PM	
	12.AM	

BREAKFAST

LUNCH

DINNER

WATER

HAPPY SCALE

MY REWARD

DAILY PLANNER

TODAY IS /

WEATHER

TODAY I AM EXCITED ABOUT

TODAY I AM GRATEFUL FOR

TODAY'S TOP PRIORITY

1.

2.

3.

TO DO LIST

TODAY'S SCHEDULE

PLAN		TRACK
	5.AM	
	6.AM	
	7.AM	
	8.AM	
	9.AM	
	10.AM	
	11.AM	
	12.PM	
	1.PM	
	3.PM	
	4.PM	
	5.PM	
	6.PM	
	7.PM	
	8.PM	
	9.PM	
	10.PM	
	11.PM	
	12.AM	

BREAKFAST

LUNCH

DINNER

WATER

HAPPY SCALE

MY REWARD

DAILY PLANNER

TODAY IS /

WEATHER

TODAY I AM EXCITED ABOUT

TODAY I AM GRATEFUL FOR

TODAY'S TOP PRIORITY

1.

2.

3.

TO DO LIST

TODAY'S SCHEDULE

PLAN		TRACK
	5.AM	
	6.AM	
	7.AM	
	8.AM	
	9.AM	
	10.AM	
	11.AM	
	12.PM	
	1.PM	
	3.PM	
	4.PM	
	5.PM	
	6.PM	
	7.PM	
	8.PM	
	9.PM	
	10.PM	
	11.PM	
	12.AM	

BREAKFAST

LUNCH

DINNER

WATER

HAPPY SCALE

MY REWARD

DAILY PLANNER

TODAY IS /

WEATHER

TODAY I AM EXCITED ABOUT

TODAY I AM GRATEFUL FOR

TODAY'S TOP PRIORITY

1.

2.

3.

TO DO LIST

TODAY'S SCHEDULE

PLAN		TRACK
	5.AM	
	6.AM	
	7.AM	
	8.AM	
	9.AM	
	10.AM	
	11.AM	
	12.PM	
	1.PM	
	3.PM	
	4.PM	
	5.PM	
	6.PM	
	7.PM	
	8.PM	
	9.PM	
	10.PM	
	11.PM	
	12.AM	

BREAKFAST

LUNCH

DINNER

WATER

HAPPY SCALE

MY REWARD

DAILY PLANNER

TODAY IS /

WEATHER

TODAY I AM EXCITED ABOUT

TODAY I AM GRATEFUL FOR

TODAY'S TOP PRIORITY

1.

2.

3.

TO DO LIST

TODAY'S SCHEDULE

PLAN		TRACK
	5.AM	
	6.AM	
	7.AM	
	8.AM	
	9.AM	
	10.AM	
	11.AM	
	12.PM	
	1.PM	
	3.PM	
	4.PM	
	5.PM	
	6.PM	
	7.PM	
	8.PM	
	9.PM	
	10.PM	
	11.PM	
	12.AM	

BREAKFAST

LUNCH

DINNER

WATER

HAPPY SCALE

MY REWARD

DAILY PLANNER

TODAY IS /

WEATHER

TODAY I AM EXCITED ABOUT

TODAY I AM GRATEFUL FOR

TODAY'S TOP PRIORITY

1.

2.

3.

TO DO LIST

TODAY'S SCHEDULE

PLAN		TRACK
	5.AM	
	6.AM	
	7.AM	
	8.AM	
	9.AM	
	10.AM	
	11.AM	
	12.PM	
	1.PM	
	3.PM	
	4.PM	
	5.PM	
	6.PM	
	7.PM	
	8.PM	
	9.PM	
	10.PM	
	11.PM	
	12.AM	

BREAKFAST

LUNCH

DINNER

WATER

HAPPY SCALE

MY REWARD

DAILY PLANNER

TODAY IS /

WEATHER

TODAY I AM EXCITED ABOUT

TODAY I AM GRATEFUL FOR

TODAY'S TOP PRIORITY

1.

2.

3.

TO DO LIST

TODAY'S SCHEDULE

PLAN		TRACK
	5.AM	
	6.AM	
	7.AM	
	8.AM	
	9.AM	
	10.AM	
	11.AM	
	12.PM	
	1.PM	
	3.PM	
	4.PM	
	5.PM	
	6.PM	
	7.PM	
	8.PM	
	9.PM	
	10.PM	
	11.PM	
	12.AM	

BREAKFAST

LUNCH

DINNER

WATER

HAPPY SCALE

MY REWARD

DAILY PLANNER

TODAY IS /

WEATHER

TODAY I AM EXCITED ABOUT

TODAY I AM GRATEFUL FOR

TODAY'S TOP PRIORITY

1.

2.

3.

TO DO LIST

TODAY'S SCHEDULE

PLAN		TRACK
	5.AM	
	6.AM	
	7.AM	
	8.AM	
	9.AM	
	10.AM	
	11.AM	
	12.PM	
	1.PM	
	3.PM	
	4.PM	
	5.PM	
	6.PM	
	7.PM	
	8.PM	
	9.PM	
	10.PM	
	11.PM	
	12.AM	

BREAKFAST

LUNCH

DINNER

WATER

HAPPY SCALE

MY REWARD

DAILY PLANNER

TODAY IS /

WEATHER

TODAY I AM EXCITED ABOUT

TODAY I AM GRATEFUL FOR

TODAY'S TOP PRIORITY

1.

2.

3.

TO DO LIST

TODAY'S SCHEDULE

PLAN		TRACK
	5.AM	
	6.AM	
	7.AM	
	8.AM	
	9.AM	
	10.AM	
	11.AM	
	12.PM	
	1.PM	
	3.PM	
	4.PM	
	5.PM	
	6.PM	
	7.PM	
	8.PM	
	9.PM	
	10.PM	
	11.PM	
	12.AM	

BREAKFAST

LUNCH

DINNER

WATER

HAPPY SCALE

MY REWARD

DAILY PLANNER

TODAY IS /

WEATHER

TODAY I AM EXCITED ABOUT

TODAY I AM GRATEFUL FOR

TODAY'S TOP PRIORITY

1.

2.

3.

TO DO LIST

TODAY'S SCHEDULE

PLAN		TRACK
	5.AM	
	6.AM	
	7.AM	
	8.AM	
	9.AM	
	10.AM	
	11.AM	
	12.PM	
	1.PM	
	3.PM	
	4.PM	
	5.PM	
	6.PM	
	7.PM	
	8.PM	
	9.PM	
	10.PM	
	11.PM	
	12.AM	

BREAKFAST

LUNCH

DINNER

WATER

HAPPY SCALE

MY REWARD

DAILY PLANNER

TODAY IS /

WEATHER

TODAY I AM EXCITED ABOUT

TODAY I AM GRATEFUL FOR

TODAY'S TOP PRIORITY

1.

2.

3.

TO DO LIST

TODAY'S SCHEDULE

PLAN		TRACK
	5.AM	
	6.AM	
	7.AM	
	8.AM	
	9.AM	
	10.AM	
	11.AM	
	12.PM	
	1.PM	
	3.PM	
	4.PM	
	5.PM	
	6.PM	
	7.PM	
	8.PM	
	9.PM	
	10.PM	
	11.PM	
	12.AM	

BREAKFAST

LUNCH

DINNER

WATER

HAPPY SCALE

MY REWARD

DAILY PLANNER

TODAY IS /

WEATHER

TODAY I AM EXCITED ABOUT

TODAY I AM GRATEFUL FOR

TODAY'S TOP PRIORITY

1.

2.

3.

TO DO LIST

TODAY'S SCHEDULE

PLAN		TRACK
	5.AM	
	6.AM	
	7.AM	
	8.AM	
	9.AM	
	10.AM	
	11.AM	
	12.PM	
	1.PM	
	3.PM	
	4.PM	
	5.PM	
	6.PM	
	7.PM	
	8.PM	
	9.PM	
	10.PM	
	11.PM	
	12.AM	

BREAKFAST

LUNCH

DINNER

WATER

HAPPY SCALE

MY REWARD

DAILY PLANNER

TODAY IS /

WEATHER

TODAY I AM EXCITED ABOUT

TODAY I AM GRATEFUL FOR

TODAY'S TOP PRIORITY

1.
2.
3.

TO DO LIST

TODAY'S SCHEDULE

PLAN		TRACK
	5.AM	
	6.AM	
	7.AM	
	8.AM	
	9.AM	
	10.AM	
	11.AM	
	12.PM	
	1.PM	
	3.PM	
	4.PM	
	5.PM	
	6.PM	
	7.PM	
	8.PM	
	9.PM	
	10.PM	
	11.PM	
	12.AM	

BREAKFAST

LUNCH

DINNER

WATER

HAPPY SCALE

MY REWARD

DAILY PLANNER

TODAY IS /

WEATHER

TODAY I AM EXCITED ABOUT

TODAY I AM GRATEFUL FOR

TODAY'S TOP PRIORITY

1.

2.

3.

TO DO LIST

TODAY'S SCHEDULE

PLAN		TRACK
	5.AM	
	6.AM	
	7.AM	
	8.AM	
	9.AM	
	10.AM	
	11.AM	
	12.PM	
	1.PM	
	3.PM	
	4.PM	
	5.PM	
	6.PM	
	7.PM	
	8.PM	
	9.PM	
	10.PM	
	11.PM	
	12.AM	

BREAKFAST

LUNCH

DINNER

WATER

HAPPY SCALE

MY REWARD

DAILY PLANNER

TODAY IS /

WEATHER

TODAY I AM EXCITED ABOUT

TODAY I AM GRATEFUL FOR

TODAY'S TOP PRIORITY

1.

2.

3.

TO DO LIST

TODAY'S SCHEDULE

PLAN		TRACK
	5.AM	
	6.AM	
	7.AM	
	8.AM	
	9.AM	
	10.AM	
	11.AM	
	12.PM	
	1.PM	
	3.PM	
	4.PM	
	5.PM	
	6.PM	
	7.PM	
	8.PM	
	9.PM	
	10.PM	
	11.PM	
	12.AM	

BREAKFAST

LUNCH

DINNER

WATER

HAPPY SCALE

MY REWARD

DAILY PLANNER

TODAY IS /

WEATHER

TODAY I AM EXCITED ABOUT

TODAY I AM GRATEFUL FOR

TODAY'S TOP PRIORITY

1.

2.

3.

TO DO LIST

TODAY'S SCHEDULE

PLAN		TRACK
	5.AM	
	6.AM	
	7.AM	
	8.AM	
	9.AM	
	10.AM	
	11.AM	
	12.PM	
	1.PM	
	3.PM	
	4.PM	
	5.PM	
	6.PM	
	7.PM	
	8.PM	
	9.PM	
	10.PM	
	11.PM	
	12.AM	

BREAKFAST

LUNCH

DINNER

WATER

HAPPY SCALE

MY REWARD

DAILY PLANNER

TODAY IS /

WEATHER

TODAY I AM EXCITED ABOUT

TODAY I AM GRATEFUL FOR

TODAY'S TOP PRIORITY

1.

2.

3.

TO DO LIST

TODAY'S SCHEDULE

PLAN		TRACK
	5.AM	
	6.AM	
	7.AM	
	8.AM	
	9.AM	
	10.AM	
	11.AM	
	12.PM	
	1.PM	
	3.PM	
	4.PM	
	5.PM	
	6.PM	
	7.PM	
	8.PM	
	9.PM	
	10.PM	
	11.PM	
	12.AM	

BREAKFAST

LUNCH

DINNER

WATER

HAPPY SCALE

MY REWARD

DAILY PLANNER

TODAY IS /

WEATHER

TODAY I AM EXCITED ABOUT

TODAY I AM GRATEFUL FOR

TODAY'S TOP PRIORITY

1.

2.

3.

TO DO LIST

TODAY'S SCHEDULE

PLAN		TRACK
	5.AM	
	6.AM	
	7.AM	
	8.AM	
	9.AM	
	10.AM	
	11.AM	
	12.PM	
	1.PM	
	3.PM	
	4.PM	
	5.PM	
	6.PM	
	7.PM	
	8.PM	
	9.PM	
	10.PM	
	11.PM	
	12.AM	

BREAKFAST

LUNCH

DINNER

WATER

HAPPY SCALE

MY REWARD

DAILY PLANNER

TODAY IS /

WEATHER

TODAY I AM EXCITED ABOUT

TODAY I AM GRATEFUL FOR

TODAY'S TOP PRIORITY

1.

2.

3.

TO DO LIST

TODAY'S SCHEDULE

PLAN		TRACK
	5.AM	
	6.AM	
	7.AM	
	8.AM	
	9.AM	
	10.AM	
	11.AM	
	12.PM	
	1.PM	
	3.PM	
	4.PM	
	5.PM	
	6.PM	
	7.PM	
	8.PM	
	9.PM	
	10.PM	
	11.PM	
	12.AM	

BREAKFAST

LUNCH

DINNER

WATER

HAPPY SCALE

MY REWARD

DAILY PLANNER

TODAY IS /

WEATHER

TODAY I AM EXCITED ABOUT

TODAY I AM GRATEFUL FOR

TODAY'S TOP PRIORITY

1.

2.

3.

TO DO LIST

TODAY'S SCHEDULE

PLAN		TRACK
	5.AM	
	6.AM	
	7.AM	
	8.AM	
	9.AM	
	10.AM	
	11.AM	
	12.PM	
	1.PM	
	3.PM	
	4.PM	
	5.PM	
	6.PM	
	7.PM	
	8.PM	
	9.PM	
	10.PM	
	11.PM	
	12.AM	

BREAKFAST

LUNCH

DINNER

WATER

HAPPY SCALE

MY REWARD

DAILY PLANNER

TODAY IS /

WEATHER

TODAY I AM EXCITED ABOUT

TODAY I AM GRATEFUL FOR

TODAY'S TOP PRIORITY

1.
2.
3.

TO DO LIST

TODAY'S SCHEDULE

PLAN		TRACK
	5.AM	
	6.AM	
	7.AM	
	8.AM	
	9.AM	
	10.AM	
	11.AM	
	12.PM	
	1.PM	
	3.PM	
	4.PM	
	5.PM	
	6.PM	
	7.PM	
	8.PM	
	9.PM	
	10.PM	
	11.PM	
	12.AM	

BREAKFAST

LUNCH

DINNER

WATER

HAPPY SCALE

MY REWARD

DAILY PLANNER

TODAY IS /

WEATHER

TODAY I AM EXCITED ABOUT

TODAY I AM GRATEFUL FOR

TODAY'S TOP PRIORITY

1.

2.

3.

TO DO LIST

TODAY'S SCHEDULE

PLAN		TRACK
	5.AM	
	6.AM	
	7.AM	
	8.AM	
	9.AM	
	10.AM	
	11.AM	
	12.PM	
	1.PM	
	3.PM	
	4.PM	
	5.PM	
	6.PM	
	7.PM	
	8.PM	
	9.PM	
	10.PM	
	11.PM	
	12.AM	

BREAKFAST

LUNCH

DINNER

WATER

HAPPY SCALE

MY REWARD

DAILY PLANNER

TODAY IS /

WEATHER

TODAY I AM EXCITED ABOUT

TODAY I AM GRATEFUL FOR

TODAY'S TOP PRIORITY

1.

2.

3.

TO DO LIST

TODAY'S SCHEDULE

PLAN		TRACK
	5.AM	
	6.AM	
	7.AM	
	8.AM	
	9.AM	
	10.AM	
	11.AM	
	12.PM	
	1.PM	
	3.PM	
	4.PM	
	5.PM	
	6.PM	
	7.PM	
	8.PM	
	9.PM	
	10.PM	
	11.PM	
	12.AM	

BREAKFAST

LUNCH

DINNER

WATER

HAPPY SCALE

MY REWARD

DAILY PLANNER

TODAY IS /

WEATHER

TODAY I AM EXCITED ABOUT

TODAY I AM GRATEFUL FOR

TODAY'S TOP PRIORITY

1.

2.

3.

TO DO LIST

TODAY'S SCHEDULE

PLAN		TRACK
	5.AM	
	6.AM	
	7.AM	
	8.AM	
	9.AM	
	10.AM	
	11.AM	
	12.PM	
	1.PM	
	3.PM	
	4.PM	
	5.PM	
	6.PM	
	7.PM	
	8.PM	
	9.PM	
	10.PM	
	11.PM	
	12.AM	

BREAKFAST

LUNCH

DINNER

WATER

HAPPY SCALE

MY REWARD

DAILY PLANNER

TODAY IS /

WEATHER

TODAY I AM EXCITED ABOUT

TODAY I AM GRATEFUL FOR

TODAY'S TOP PRIORITY

1.
2.
3.

TO DO LIST

TODAY'S SCHEDULE

PLAN		TRACK
	5.AM	
	6.AM	
	7.AM	
	8.AM	
	9.AM	
	10.AM	
	11.AM	
	12.PM	
	1.PM	
	3.PM	
	4.PM	
	5.PM	
	6.PM	
	7.PM	
	8.PM	
	9.PM	
	10.PM	
	11.PM	
	12.AM	

BREAKFAST

LUNCH

DINNER

WATER

HAPPY SCALE

MY REWARD

DAILY PLANNER

TODAY IS /

WEATHER

TODAY I AM EXCITED ABOUT

TODAY I AM GRATEFUL FOR

TODAY'S TOP PRIORITY

1.

2.

3.

TO DO LIST

TODAY'S SCHEDULE

PLAN		TRACK
	5.AM	
	6.AM	
	7.AM	
	8.AM	
	9.AM	
	10.AM	
	11.AM	
	12.PM	
	1.PM	
	3.PM	
	4.PM	
	5.PM	
	6.PM	
	7.PM	
	8.PM	
	9.PM	
	10.PM	
	11.PM	
	12.AM	

BREAKFAST

LUNCH

DINNER

WATER

HAPPY SCALE

MY REWARD

DAILY PLANNER

TODAY IS /

WEATHER

TODAY I AM EXCITED ABOUT

TODAY I AM GRATEFUL FOR

TODAY'S TOP PRIORITY

1.

2.

3.

TO DO LIST

TODAY'S SCHEDULE

PLAN		TRACK
	5.AM	
	6.AM	
	7.AM	
	8.AM	
	9.AM	
	10.AM	
	11.AM	
	12.PM	
	1.PM	
	3.PM	
	4.PM	
	5.PM	
	6.PM	
	7.PM	
	8.PM	
	9.PM	
	10.PM	
	11.PM	
	12.AM	

BREAKFAST

LUNCH

DINNER

WATER

HAPPY SCALE

MY REWARD

DAILY PLANNER

TODAY IS /

WEATHER

TODAY I AM EXCITED ABOUT

TODAY I AM GRATEFUL FOR

TODAY'S TOP PRIORITY

1.
2.
3.

TO DO LIST

TODAY'S SCHEDULE

PLAN		TRACK
	5.AM	
	6.AM	
	7.AM	
	8.AM	
	9.AM	
	10.AM	
	11.AM	
	12.PM	
	1.PM	
	3.PM	
	4.PM	
	5.PM	
	6.PM	
	7.PM	
	8.PM	
	9.PM	
	10.PM	
	11.PM	
	12.AM	

BREAKFAST

LUNCH

DINNER

WATER

HAPPY SCALE

MY REWARD

DAILY PLANNER

TODAY IS /

WEATHER

TODAY I AM EXCITED ABOUT

TODAY I AM GRATEFUL FOR

TODAY'S TOP PRIORITY

1.
2.
3.

TO DO LIST

TODAY'S SCHEDULE

PLAN		TRACK
	5.AM	
	6.AM	
	7.AM	
	8.AM	
	9.AM	
	10.AM	
	11.AM	
	12.PM	
	1.PM	
	3.PM	
	4.PM	
	5.PM	
	6.PM	
	7.PM	
	8.PM	
	9.PM	
	10.PM	
	11.PM	
	12.AM	

BREAKFAST

LUNCH

DINNER

WATER

HAPPY SCALE

MY REWARD

DAILY PLANNER

TODAY IS /

WEATHER

TODAY I AM EXCITED ABOUT

TODAY I AM GRATEFUL FOR

TODAY'S TOP PRIORITY

1.

2.

3.

TO DO LIST

TODAY'S SCHEDULE

PLAN		TRACK
	5.AM	
	6.AM	
	7.AM	
	8.AM	
	9.AM	
	10.AM	
	11.AM	
	12.PM	
	1.PM	
	3.PM	
	4.PM	
	5.PM	
	6.PM	
	7.PM	
	8.PM	
	9.PM	
	10.PM	
	11.PM	
	12.AM	

BREAKFAST

LUNCH

DINNER

WATER

HAPPY SCALE

MY REWARD

DAILY PLANNER

TODAY IS /

WEATHER

TODAY I AM EXCITED ABOUT

TODAY I AM GRATEFUL FOR

TODAY'S TOP PRIORITY

1.

2.

3.

TO DO LIST

TODAY'S SCHEDULE

PLAN		TRACK
	5.AM	
	6.AM	
	7.AM	
	8.AM	
	9.AM	
	10.AM	
	11.AM	
	12.PM	
	1.PM	
	3.PM	
	4.PM	
	5.PM	
	6.PM	
	7.PM	
	8.PM	
	9.PM	
	10.PM	
	11.PM	
	12.AM	

BREAKFAST

LUNCH

DINNER

WATER

HAPPY SCALE

MY REWARD

DAILY PLANNER

TODAY IS /

WEATHER

TODAY I AM EXCITED ABOUT

TODAY I AM GRATEFUL FOR

TODAY'S TOP PRIORITY

1.

2.

3.

TO DO LIST

TODAY'S SCHEDULE

PLAN		TRACK
	5.AM	
	6.AM	
	7.AM	
	8.AM	
	9.AM	
	10.AM	
	11.AM	
	12.PM	
	1.PM	
	3.PM	
	4.PM	
	5.PM	
	6.PM	
	7.PM	
	8.PM	
	9.PM	
	10.PM	
	11.PM	
	12.AM	

BREAKFAST

LUNCH

DINNER

WATER

HAPPY SCALE

MY REWARD

DAILY PLANNER

TODAY IS /

WEATHER

TODAY I AM EXCITED ABOUT

TODAY I AM GRATEFUL FOR

TODAY'S TOP PRIORITY

1.

2.

3.

TO DO LIST

TODAY'S SCHEDULE

PLAN		TRACK
	5.AM	
	6.AM	
	7.AM	
	8.AM	
	9.AM	
	10.AM	
	11.AM	
	12.PM	
	1.PM	
	3.PM	
	4.PM	
	5.PM	
	6.PM	
	7.PM	
	8.PM	
	9.PM	
	10.PM	
	11.PM	
	12.AM	

BREAKFAST

LUNCH

DINNER

WATER

HAPPY SCALE

MY REWARD

DAILY PLANNER

TODAY IS /

WEATHER

TODAY I AM EXCITED ABOUT

TODAY I AM GRATEFUL FOR

TODAY'S TOP PRIORITY

1.

2.

3.

TO DO LIST

TODAY'S SCHEDULE

PLAN		TRACK
	5.AM	
	6.AM	
	7.AM	
	8.AM	
	9.AM	
	10.AM	
	11.AM	
	12.PM	
	1.PM	
	3.PM	
	4.PM	
	5.PM	
	6.PM	
	7.PM	
	8.PM	
	9.PM	
	10.PM	
	11.PM	
	12.AM	

BREAKFAST

LUNCH

DINNER

WATER

HAPPY SCALE

MY REWARD

DAILY PLANNER

TODAY IS /

WEATHER

TODAY I AM EXCITED ABOUT

TODAY I AM GRATEFUL FOR

TODAY'S TOP PRIORITY

1.

2.

3.

TO DO LIST

TODAY'S SCHEDULE

PLAN		TRACK
	5.AM	
	6.AM	
	7.AM	
	8.AM	
	9.AM	
	10.AM	
	11.AM	
	12.PM	
	1.PM	
	3.PM	
	4.PM	
	5.PM	
	6.PM	
	7.PM	
	8.PM	
	9.PM	
	10.PM	
	11.PM	
	12.AM	

BREAKFAST

LUNCH

DINNER

WATER

HAPPY SCALE

MY REWARD

DAILY PLANNER

TODAY IS /

WEATHER

TODAY I AM EXCITED ABOUT

TODAY I AM GRATEFUL FOR

TODAY'S TOP PRIORITY

1.

2.

3.

TO DO LIST

TODAY'S SCHEDULE

PLAN		TRACK
	5.AM	
	6.AM	
	7.AM	
	8.AM	
	9.AM	
	10.AM	
	11.AM	
	12.PM	
	1.PM	
	3.PM	
	4.PM	
	5.PM	
	6.PM	
	7.PM	
	8.PM	
	9.PM	
	10.PM	
	11.PM	
	12.AM	

BREAKFAST

LUNCH

DINNER

WATER

HAPPY SCALE

MY REWARD

DAILY PLANNER

TODAY IS /

WEATHER

TODAY I AM EXCITED ABOUT

TODAY I AM GRATEFUL FOR

TODAY'S TOP PRIORITY

1.

2.

3.

TO DO LIST

TODAY'S SCHEDULE

PLAN		TRACK
	5.AM	
	6.AM	
	7.AM	
	8.AM	
	9.AM	
	10.AM	
	11.AM	
	12.PM	
	1.PM	
	3.PM	
	4.PM	
	5.PM	
	6.PM	
	7.PM	
	8.PM	
	9.PM	
	10.PM	
	11.PM	
	12.AM	

BREAKFAST

LUNCH

DINNER

WATER

HAPPY SCALE

MY REWARD

DAILY PLANNER

TODAY IS /

WEATHER

TODAY I AM EXCITED ABOUT

TODAY I AM GRATEFUL FOR

TODAY'S TOP PRIORITY

1.

2.

3.

TO DO LIST

TODAY'S SCHEDULE

PLAN		TRACK
	5.AM	
	6.AM	
	7.AM	
	8.AM	
	9.AM	
	10.AM	
	11.AM	
	12.PM	
	1.PM	
	3.PM	
	4.PM	
	5.PM	
	6.PM	
	7.PM	
	8.PM	
	9.PM	
	10.PM	
	11.PM	
	12.AM	

BREAKFAST

LUNCH

DINNER

WATER

HAPPY SCALE

MY REWARD

DAILY PLANNER

TODAY IS /

WEATHER

TODAY I AM EXCITED ABOUT

TODAY I AM GRATEFUL FOR

TODAY'S TOP PRIORITY

1.

2.

3.

TO DO LIST

TODAY'S SCHEDULE

PLAN		TRACK
	5.AM	
	6.AM	
	7.AM	
	8.AM	
	9.AM	
	10.AM	
	11.AM	
	12.PM	
	1.PM	
	3.PM	
	4.PM	
	5.PM	
	6.PM	
	7.PM	
	8.PM	
	9.PM	
	10.PM	
	11.PM	
	12.AM	

BREAKFAST

LUNCH

DINNER

WATER

HAPPY SCALE

MY REWARD

DAILY PLANNER

TODAY IS /

WEATHER

TODAY I AM EXCITED ABOUT

TODAY I AM GRATEFUL FOR

TODAY'S TOP PRIORITY

1.

2.

3.

TO DO LIST

TODAY'S SCHEDULE

PLAN		TRACK
	5.AM	
	6.AM	
	7.AM	
	8.AM	
	9.AM	
	10.AM	
	11.AM	
	12.PM	
	1.PM	
	3.PM	
	4.PM	
	5.PM	
	6.PM	
	7.PM	
	8.PM	
	9.PM	
	10.PM	
	11.PM	
	12.AM	

BREAKFAST

LUNCH

DINNER

WATER

HAPPY SCALE

MY REWARD

DAILY PLANNER

TODAY IS /

WEATHER

TODAY I AM EXCITED ABOUT

TODAY I AM GRATEFUL FOR

TODAY'S TOP PRIORITY

1.

2.

3.

TO DO LIST

TODAY'S SCHEDULE

PLAN		TRACK
	5.AM	
	6.AM	
	7.AM	
	8.AM	
	9.AM	
	10.AM	
	11.AM	
	12.PM	
	1.PM	
	3.PM	
	4.PM	
	5.PM	
	6.PM	
	7.PM	
	8.PM	
	9.PM	
	10.PM	
	11.PM	
	12.AM	

BREAKFAST

LUNCH

DINNER

WATER

HAPPY SCALE

MY REWARD

DAILY PLANNER

TODAY IS /

WEATHER

TODAY I AM EXCITED ABOUT

TODAY I AM GRATEFUL FOR

TODAY'S TOP PRIORITY

1.

2.

3.

TO DO LIST

TODAY'S SCHEDULE

PLAN		TRACK
	5.AM	
	6.AM	
	7.AM	
	8.AM	
	9.AM	
	10.AM	
	11.AM	
	12.PM	
	1.PM	
	3.PM	
	4.PM	
	5.PM	
	6.PM	
	7.PM	
	8.PM	
	9.PM	
	10.PM	
	11.PM	
	12.AM	

BREAKFAST

LUNCH

DINNER

WATER

HAPPY SCALE

MY REWARD

DAILY PLANNER

TODAY IS /

WEATHER

TODAY I AM EXCITED ABOUT

TODAY I AM GRATEFUL FOR

TODAY'S TOP PRIORITY

1.

2.

3.

TO DO LIST

TODAY'S SCHEDULE

PLAN		TRACK
	5.AM	
	6.AM	
	7.AM	
	8.AM	
	9.AM	
	10.AM	
	11.AM	
	12.PM	
	1.PM	
	3.PM	
	4.PM	
	5.PM	
	6.PM	
	7.PM	
	8.PM	
	9.PM	
	10.PM	
	11.PM	
	12.AM	

BREAKFAST

LUNCH

DINNER

WATER

HAPPY SCALE

MY REWARD

DAILY PLANNER

TODAY IS /

WEATHER

TODAY I AM EXCITED ABOUT

TODAY I AM GRATEFUL FOR

TODAY'S TOP PRIORITY

1.

2.

3.

TO DO LIST

TODAY'S SCHEDULE

PLAN		TRACK
	5.AM	
	6.AM	
	7.AM	
	8.AM	
	9.AM	
	10.AM	
	11.AM	
	12.PM	
	1.PM	
	3.PM	
	4.PM	
	5.PM	
	6.PM	
	7.PM	
	8.PM	
	9.PM	
	10.PM	
	11.PM	
	12.AM	

BREAKFAST

LUNCH

DINNER

WATER

HAPPY SCALE

MY REWARD

DAILY PLANNER

TODAY IS /

WEATHER

TODAY I AM EXCITED ABOUT

TODAY I AM GRATEFUL FOR

TODAY'S TOP PRIORITY

1.

2.

3.

TO DO LIST

TODAY'S SCHEDULE

PLAN		TRACK
	5.AM	
	6.AM	
	7.AM	
	8.AM	
	9.AM	
	10.AM	
	11.AM	
	12.PM	
	1.PM	
	3.PM	
	4.PM	
	5.PM	
	6.PM	
	7.PM	
	8.PM	
	9.PM	
	10.PM	
	11.PM	
	12.AM	

BREAKFAST

LUNCH

DINNER

WATER

HAPPY SCALE

MY REWARD

DAILY PLANNER

TODAY IS /

WEATHER

TODAY I AM EXCITED ABOUT

TODAY I AM GRATEFUL FOR

TODAY'S TOP PRIORITY

1.

2.

3.

TO DO LIST

TODAY'S SCHEDULE

PLAN		TRACK
	5.AM	
	6.AM	
	7.AM	
	8.AM	
	9.AM	
	10.AM	
	11.AM	
	12.PM	
	1.PM	
	3.PM	
	4.PM	
	5.PM	
	6.PM	
	7.PM	
	8.PM	
	9.PM	
	10.PM	
	11.PM	
	12.AM	

BREAKFAST

LUNCH

DINNER

WATER

HAPPY SCALE

MY REWARD

DAILY PLANNER

TODAY IS /

WEATHER

TODAY I AM EXCITED ABOUT

TODAY I AM GRATEFUL FOR

TODAY'S TOP PRIORITY

1.

2.

3.

TO DO LIST

TODAY'S SCHEDULE

PLAN		TRACK
	5.AM	
	6.AM	
	7.AM	
	8.AM	
	9.AM	
	10.AM	
	11.AM	
	12.PM	
	1.PM	
	3.PM	
	4.PM	
	5.PM	
	6.PM	
	7.PM	
	8.PM	
	9.PM	
	10.PM	
	11.PM	
	12.AM	

BREAKFAST

LUNCH

DINNER

WATER

HAPPY SCALE

MY REWARD

DAILY PLANNER

TODAY IS /

WEATHER

TODAY I AM EXCITED ABOUT

TODAY I AM GRATEFUL FOR

TODAY'S TOP PRIORITY

1.

2.

3.

TO DO LIST

TODAY'S SCHEDULE

PLAN		TRACK
	5.AM	
	6.AM	
	7.AM	
	8.AM	
	9.AM	
	10.AM	
	11.AM	
	12.PM	
	1.PM	
	3.PM	
	4.PM	
	5.PM	
	6.PM	
	7.PM	
	8.PM	
	9.PM	
	10.PM	
	11.PM	
	12.AM	

BREAKFAST

LUNCH

DINNER

WATER

HAPPY SCALE

MY REWARD

DAILY PLANNER

TODAY IS /

WEATHER

TODAY I AM EXCITED ABOUT

TODAY I AM GRATEFUL FOR

TODAY'S TOP PRIORITY

1.

2.

3.

TO DO LIST

TODAY'S SCHEDULE

PLAN		TRACK
	5.AM	
	6.AM	
	7.AM	
	8.AM	
	9.AM	
	10.AM	
	11.AM	
	12.PM	
	1.PM	
	3.PM	
	4.PM	
	5.PM	
	6.PM	
	7.PM	
	8.PM	
	9.PM	
	10.PM	
	11.PM	
	12.AM	

BREAKFAST

LUNCH

DINNER

WATER

HAPPY SCALE

MY REWARD

DAILY PLANNER

TODAY IS /

WEATHER

TODAY I AM EXCITED ABOUT

TODAY I AM GRATEFUL FOR

TODAY'S TOP PRIORITY

1.

2.

3.

TO DO LIST

TODAY'S SCHEDULE

PLAN		TRACK
	5.AM	
	6.AM	
	7.AM	
	8.AM	
	9.AM	
	10.AM	
	11.AM	
	12.PM	
	1.PM	
	3.PM	
	4.PM	
	5.PM	
	6.PM	
	7.PM	
	8.PM	
	9.PM	
	10.PM	
	11.PM	
	12.AM	

BREAKFAST

LUNCH

DINNER

WATER

HAPPY SCALE

MY REWARD

DAILY PLANNER

TODAY IS /

WEATHER

TODAY I AM EXCITED ABOUT

TODAY I AM GRATEFUL FOR

TODAY'S TOP PRIORITY

1.

2.

3.

TO DO LIST

TODAY'S SCHEDULE

PLAN		TRACK
	5.AM	
	6.AM	
	7.AM	
	8.AM	
	9.AM	
	10.AM	
	11.AM	
	12.PM	
	1.PM	
	3.PM	
	4.PM	
	5.PM	
	6.PM	
	7.PM	
	8.PM	
	9.PM	
	10.PM	
	11.PM	
	12.AM	

BREAKFAST

LUNCH

DINNER

WATER

HAPPY SCALE

MY REWARD

DAILY PLANNER

TODAY IS /

WEATHER

TODAY I AM EXCITED ABOUT

TODAY I AM GRATEFUL FOR

TODAY'S TOP PRIORITY

1.

2.

3.

TO DO LIST

TODAY'S SCHEDULE

PLAN		TRACK
	5.AM	
	6.AM	
	7.AM	
	8.AM	
	9.AM	
	10.AM	
	11.AM	
	12.PM	
	1.PM	
	3.PM	
	4.PM	
	5.PM	
	6.PM	
	7.PM	
	8.PM	
	9.PM	
	10.PM	
	11.PM	
	12.AM	

BREAKFAST

LUNCH

DINNER

WATER

HAPPY SCALE

MY REWARD

DAILY PLANNER

TODAY IS /

WEATHER

TODAY I AM EXCITED ABOUT

TODAY I AM GRATEFUL FOR

TODAY'S TOP PRIORITY

1.

2.

3.

TO DO LIST

TODAY'S SCHEDULE

PLAN		TRACK
	5.AM	
	6.AM	
	7.AM	
	8.AM	
	9.AM	
	10.AM	
	11.AM	
	12.PM	
	1.PM	
	3.PM	
	4.PM	
	5.PM	
	6.PM	
	7.PM	
	8.PM	
	9.PM	
	10.PM	
	11.PM	
	12.AM	

BREAKFAST

LUNCH

DINNER

WATER

HAPPY SCALE

MY REWARD

DAILY PLANNER

TODAY IS /

WEATHER

TODAY I AM EXCITED ABOUT

TODAY I AM GRATEFUL FOR

TODAY'S TOP PRIORITY

1.

2.

3.

TO DO LIST

TODAY'S SCHEDULE

PLAN		TRACK
	5.AM	
	6.AM	
	7.AM	
	8.AM	
	9.AM	
	10.AM	
	11.AM	
	12.PM	
	1.PM	
	3.PM	
	4.PM	
	5.PM	
	6.PM	
	7.PM	
	8.PM	
	9.PM	
	10.PM	
	11.PM	
	12.AM	

BREAKFAST

LUNCH

DINNER

WATER

HAPPY SCALE

MY REWARD

DAILY PLANNER

TODAY IS /

WEATHER

TODAY I AM EXCITED ABOUT

TODAY I AM GRATEFUL FOR

TODAY'S TOP PRIORITY

1.

2.

3.

TO DO LIST

TODAY'S SCHEDULE

PLAN		TRACK
	5.AM	
	6.AM	
	7.AM	
	8.AM	
	9.AM	
	10.AM	
	11.AM	
	12.PM	
	1.PM	
	3.PM	
	4.PM	
	5.PM	
	6.PM	
	7.PM	
	8.PM	
	9.PM	
	10.PM	
	11.PM	
	12.AM	

BREAKFAST

LUNCH

DINNER

WATER

HAPPY SCALE

MY REWARD

DAILY PLANNER

TODAY IS /

WEATHER

TODAY I AM EXCITED ABOUT

TODAY I AM GRATEFUL FOR

TODAY'S TOP PRIORITY

1.
2.
3.

TO DO LIST

TODAY'S SCHEDULE

PLAN		TRACK
	5.AM	
	6.AM	
	7.AM	
	8.AM	
	9.AM	
	10.AM	
	11.AM	
	12.PM	
	1.PM	
	3.PM	
	4.PM	
	5.PM	
	6.PM	
	7.PM	
	8.PM	
	9.PM	
	10.PM	
	11.PM	
	12.AM	

BREAKFAST

LUNCH

DINNER

WATER

HAPPY SCALE

MY REWARD

DAILY PLANNER

TODAY IS /

WEATHER

TODAY I AM EXCITED ABOUT

TODAY I AM GRATEFUL FOR

TODAY'S TOP PRIORITY

1.

2.

3.

TO DO LIST

TODAY'S SCHEDULE

PLAN		TRACK
	5.AM	
	6.AM	
	7.AM	
	8.AM	
	9.AM	
	10.AM	
	11.AM	
	12.PM	
	1.PM	
	3.PM	
	4.PM	
	5.PM	
	6.PM	
	7.PM	
	8.PM	
	9.PM	
	10.PM	
	11.PM	
	12.AM	

BREAKFAST

LUNCH

DINNER

WATER

HAPPY SCALE

MY REWARD

DAILY PLANNER

TODAY IS /

WEATHER

TODAY I AM EXCITED ABOUT

TODAY I AM GRATEFUL FOR

TODAY'S TOP PRIORITY

1.

2.

3.

TO DO LIST

TODAY'S SCHEDULE

PLAN		TRACK
	5.AM	
	6.AM	
	7.AM	
	8.AM	
	9.AM	
	10.AM	
	11.AM	
	12.PM	
	1.PM	
	3.PM	
	4.PM	
	5.PM	
	6.PM	
	7.PM	
	8.PM	
	9.PM	
	10.PM	
	11.PM	
	12.AM	

BREAKFAST

LUNCH

DINNER

WATER

HAPPY SCALE

MY REWARD

DAILY PLANNER

TODAY IS /

WEATHER

TODAY I AM EXCITED ABOUT

TODAY I AM GRATEFUL FOR

TODAY'S TOP PRIORITY

1.

2.

3.

TO DO LIST

TODAY'S SCHEDULE

PLAN		TRACK
	5.AM	
	6.AM	
	7.AM	
	8.AM	
	9.AM	
	10.AM	
	11.AM	
	12.PM	
	1.PM	
	3.PM	
	4.PM	
	5.PM	
	6.PM	
	7.PM	
	8.PM	
	9.PM	
	10.PM	
	11.PM	
	12.AM	

BREAKFAST

LUNCH

DINNER

WATER

HAPPY SCALE

MY REWARD

DAILY PLANNER

TODAY IS /

WEATHER

TODAY I AM EXCITED ABOUT

TODAY I AM GRATEFUL FOR

TODAY'S TOP PRIORITY

1.

2.

3.

TO DO LIST

TODAY'S SCHEDULE

PLAN		TRACK
	5.AM	
	6.AM	
	7.AM	
	8.AM	
	9.AM	
	10.AM	
	11.AM	
	12.PM	
	1.PM	
	3.PM	
	4.PM	
	5.PM	
	6.PM	
	7.PM	
	8.PM	
	9.PM	
	10.PM	
	11.PM	
	12.AM	

BREAKFAST

LUNCH

DINNER

WATER

HAPPY SCALE

MY REWARD

DAILY PLANNER

TODAY IS /

WEATHER

TODAY I AM EXCITED ABOUT

TODAY I AM GRATEFUL FOR

TODAY'S TOP PRIORITY

1.

2.

3.

TO DO LIST

TODAY'S SCHEDULE

PLAN		TRACK
	5.AM	
	6.AM	
	7.AM	
	8.AM	
	9.AM	
	10.AM	
	11.AM	
	12.PM	
	1.PM	
	3.PM	
	4.PM	
	5.PM	
	6.PM	
	7.PM	
	8.PM	
	9.PM	
	10.PM	
	11.PM	
	12.AM	

BREAKFAST

LUNCH

DINNER

WATER

HAPPY SCALE

MY REWARD

DAILY PLANNER

TODAY IS /

WEATHER

TODAY I AM EXCITED ABOUT

TODAY I AM GRATEFUL FOR

TODAY'S TOP PRIORITY

1.
2.
3.

TO DO LIST

TODAY'S SCHEDULE

PLAN		TRACK
	5.AM	
	6.AM	
	7.AM	
	8.AM	
	9.AM	
	10.AM	
	11.AM	
	12.PM	
	1.PM	
	3.PM	
	4.PM	
	5.PM	
	6.PM	
	7.PM	
	8.PM	
	9.PM	
	10.PM	
	11.PM	
	12.AM	

BREAKFAST

LUNCH

DINNER

WATER

HAPPY SCALE

MY REWARD

DAILY PLANNER

TODAY IS /

WEATHER

TODAY I AM EXCITED ABOUT

TODAY I AM GRATEFUL FOR

TODAY'S TOP PRIORITY

1.

2.

3.

TO DO LIST

TODAY'S SCHEDULE

PLAN		TRACK
	5.AM	
	6.AM	
	7.AM	
	8.AM	
	9.AM	
	10.AM	
	11.AM	
	12.PM	
	1.PM	
	3.PM	
	4.PM	
	5.PM	
	6.PM	
	7.PM	
	8.PM	
	9.PM	
	10.PM	
	11.PM	
	12.AM	

BREAKFAST

LUNCH

DINNER

WATER

HAPPY SCALE

MY REWARD

DAILY PLANNER

TODAY IS /

WEATHER

TODAY I AM EXCITED ABOUT

TODAY I AM GRATEFUL FOR

TODAY'S TOP PRIORITY

1.
2.
3.

TO DO LIST

TODAY'S SCHEDULE

PLAN		TRACK
	5.AM	
	6.AM	
	7.AM	
	8.AM	
	9.AM	
	10.AM	
	11.AM	
	12.PM	
	1.PM	
	3.PM	
	4.PM	
	5.PM	
	6.PM	
	7.PM	
	8.PM	
	9.PM	
	10.PM	
	11.PM	
	12.AM	

BREAKFAST

LUNCH

DINNER

WATER

HAPPY SCALE

MY REWARD

DAILY PLANNER

TODAY IS /

WEATHER

TODAY I AM EXCITED ABOUT

TODAY I AM GRATEFUL FOR

TODAY'S TOP PRIORITY

1.

2.

3.

TO DO LIST

TODAY'S SCHEDULE

PLAN		TRACK
	5.AM	
	6.AM	
	7.AM	
	8.AM	
	9.AM	
	10.AM	
	11.AM	
	12.PM	
	1.PM	
	3.PM	
	4.PM	
	5.PM	
	6.PM	
	7.PM	
	8.PM	
	9.PM	
	10.PM	
	11.PM	
	12.AM	

BREAKFAST

LUNCH

DINNER

WATER

HAPPY SCALE

MY REWARD

DAILY PLANNER

TODAY IS /

WEATHER

TODAY I AM EXCITED ABOUT

TODAY I AM GRATEFUL FOR

TODAY'S TOP PRIORITY

1.

2.

3.

TO DO LIST

TODAY'S SCHEDULE

PLAN		TRACK
	5.AM	
	6.AM	
	7.AM	
	8.AM	
	9.AM	
	10.AM	
	11.AM	
	12.PM	
	1.PM	
	3.PM	
	4.PM	
	5.PM	
	6.PM	
	7.PM	
	8.PM	
	9.PM	
	10.PM	
	11.PM	
	12.AM	

BREAKFAST

LUNCH

DINNER

WATER

HAPPY SCALE

MY REWARD

DAILY PLANNER

TODAY IS /

WEATHER

TODAY I AM EXCITED ABOUT

TODAY I AM GRATEFUL FOR

TODAY'S TOP PRIORITY

1.

2.

3.

TO DO LIST

TODAY'S SCHEDULE

PLAN		TRACK
	5.AM	
	6.AM	
	7.AM	
	8.AM	
	9.AM	
	10.AM	
	11.AM	
	12.PM	
	1.PM	
	3.PM	
	4.PM	
	5.PM	
	6.PM	
	7.PM	
	8.PM	
	9.PM	
	10.PM	
	11.PM	
	12.AM	

BREAKFAST

LUNCH

DINNER

WATER

HAPPY SCALE

MY REWARD

DAILY PLANNER

TODAY IS /

WEATHER

TODAY I AM EXCITED ABOUT

TODAY I AM GRATEFUL FOR

TODAY'S TOP PRIORITY

1.

2.

3.

TO DO LIST

TODAY'S SCHEDULE

PLAN		TRACK
	5.AM	
	6.AM	
	7.AM	
	8.AM	
	9.AM	
	10.AM	
	11.AM	
	12.PM	
	1.PM	
	3.PM	
	4.PM	
	5.PM	
	6.PM	
	7.PM	
	8.PM	
	9.PM	
	10.PM	
	11.PM	
	12.AM	

BREAKFAST

LUNCH

DINNER

WATER

HAPPY SCALE

MY REWARD

DAILY PLANNER

TODAY IS /

WEATHER

TODAY I AM EXCITED ABOUT

TODAY I AM GRATEFUL FOR

TODAY'S TOP PRIORITY

1.

2.

3.

TO DO LIST

TODAY'S SCHEDULE

PLAN		TRACK
	5.AM	
	6.AM	
	7.AM	
	8.AM	
	9.AM	
	10.AM	
	11.AM	
	12.PM	
	1.PM	
	3.PM	
	4.PM	
	5.PM	
	6.PM	
	7.PM	
	8.PM	
	9.PM	
	10.PM	
	11.PM	
	12.AM	

BREAKFAST

LUNCH

DINNER

WATER

HAPPY SCALE

MY REWARD

DAILY PLANNER

TODAY IS /

WEATHER

TODAY I AM EXCITED ABOUT

TODAY I AM GRATEFUL FOR

TODAY'S TOP PRIORITY

1.

2.

3.

TO DO LIST

TODAY'S SCHEDULE

PLAN		TRACK
	5.AM	
	6.AM	
	7.AM	
	8.AM	
	9.AM	
	10.AM	
	11.AM	
	12.PM	
	1.PM	
	3.PM	
	4.PM	
	5.PM	
	6.PM	
	7.PM	
	8.PM	
	9.PM	
	10.PM	
	11.PM	
	12.AM	

BREAKFAST

LUNCH

DINNER

WATER

HAPPY SCALE

MY REWARD

DAILY PLANNER

TODAY IS /

WEATHER

TODAY I AM EXCITED ABOUT

TODAY I AM GRATEFUL FOR

TODAY'S TOP PRIORITY

1.
2.
3.

TO DO LIST

TODAY'S SCHEDULE

PLAN		TRACK
	5.AM	
	6.AM	
	7.AM	
	8.AM	
	9.AM	
	10.AM	
	11.AM	
	12.PM	
	1.PM	
	3.PM	
	4.PM	
	5.PM	
	6.PM	
	7.PM	
	8.PM	
	9.PM	
	10.PM	
	11.PM	
	12.AM	

BREAKFAST

LUNCH

DINNER

WATER

HAPPY SCALE

MY REWARD

DAILY PLANNER

TODAY IS /

WEATHER

TODAY I AM EXCITED ABOUT

TODAY I AM GRATEFUL FOR

TODAY'S TOP PRIORITY

1.

2.

3.

TO DO LIST

TODAY'S SCHEDULE

PLAN		TRACK
	5.AM	
	6.AM	
	7.AM	
	8.AM	
	9.AM	
	10.AM	
	11.AM	
	12.PM	
	1.PM	
	3.PM	
	4.PM	
	5.PM	
	6.PM	
	7.PM	
	8.PM	
	9.PM	
	10.PM	
	11.PM	
	12.AM	

BREAKFAST

LUNCH

DINNER

WATER

HAPPY SCALE

MY REWARD

DAILY PLANNER

TODAY IS /

WEATHER

TODAY I AM EXCITED ABOUT

TODAY I AM GRATEFUL FOR

TODAY'S TOP PRIORITY

1.

2.

3.

TO DO LIST

TODAY'S SCHEDULE

PLAN		TRACK
	5.AM	
	6.AM	
	7.AM	
	8.AM	
	9.AM	
	10.AM	
	11.AM	
	12.PM	
	1.PM	
	3.PM	
	4.PM	
	5.PM	
	6.PM	
	7.PM	
	8.PM	
	9.PM	
	10.PM	
	11.PM	
	12.AM	

BREAKFAST

LUNCH

DINNER

WATER

HAPPY SCALE

MY REWARD

DAILY PLANNER

TODAY IS /

WEATHER

TODAY I AM EXCITED ABOUT

TODAY I AM GRATEFUL FOR

TODAY'S TOP PRIORITY

1.

2.

3.

TO DO LIST

TODAY'S SCHEDULE

PLAN		TRACK
	5.AM	
	6.AM	
	7.AM	
	8.AM	
	9.AM	
	10.AM	
	11.AM	
	12.PM	
	1.PM	
	3.PM	
	4.PM	
	5.PM	
	6.PM	
	7.PM	
	8.PM	
	9.PM	
	10.PM	
	11.PM	
	12.AM	

BREAKFAST

LUNCH

DINNER

WATER

HAPPY SCALE

MY REWARD

DAILY PLANNER

TODAY IS /

WEATHER

TODAY I AM EXCITED ABOUT

TODAY I AM GRATEFUL FOR

TODAY'S TOP PRIORITY

1.

2.

3.

TO DO LIST

TODAY'S SCHEDULE

PLAN		TRACK
	5.AM	
	6.AM	
	7.AM	
	8.AM	
	9.AM	
	10.AM	
	11.AM	
	12.PM	
	1.PM	
	3.PM	
	4.PM	
	5.PM	
	6.PM	
	7.PM	
	8.PM	
	9.PM	
	10.PM	
	11.PM	
	12.AM	

BREAKFAST

LUNCH

DINNER

WATER

HAPPY SCALE

MY REWARD

DAILY PLANNER

TODAY IS /

WEATHER

TODAY I AM EXCITED ABOUT

TODAY I AM GRATEFUL FOR

TODAY'S TOP PRIORITY

1.

2.

3.

TO DO LIST

TODAY'S SCHEDULE

PLAN		TRACK
	5.AM	
	6.AM	
	7.AM	
	8.AM	
	9.AM	
	10.AM	
	11.AM	
	12.PM	
	1.PM	
	3.PM	
	4.PM	
	5.PM	
	6.PM	
	7.PM	
	8.PM	
	9.PM	
	10.PM	
	11.PM	
	12.AM	

BREAKFAST

LUNCH

DINNER

WATER

HAPPY SCALE

MY REWARD

DAILY PLANNER

TODAY IS /

WEATHER

TODAY I AM EXCITED ABOUT

TODAY I AM GRATEFUL FOR

TODAY'S TOP PRIORITY

1.

2.

3.

TO DO LIST

TODAY'S SCHEDULE

PLAN		TRACK
	5.AM	
	6.AM	
	7.AM	
	8.AM	
	9.AM	
	10.AM	
	11.AM	
	12.PM	
	1.PM	
	3.PM	
	4.PM	
	5.PM	
	6.PM	
	7.PM	
	8.PM	
	9.PM	
	10.PM	
	11.PM	
	12.AM	

BREAKFAST

LUNCH

DINNER

WATER

HAPPY SCALE

MY REWARD

DAILY PLANNER

TODAY IS /

WEATHER

TODAY I AM EXCITED ABOUT

TODAY I AM GRATEFUL FOR

TODAY'S TOP PRIORITY

1.

2.

3.

TO DO LIST

TODAY'S SCHEDULE

PLAN		TRACK
	5.AM	
	6.AM	
	7.AM	
	8.AM	
	9.AM	
	10.AM	
	11.AM	
	12.PM	
	1.PM	
	3.PM	
	4.PM	
	5.PM	
	6.PM	
	7.PM	
	8.PM	
	9.PM	
	10.PM	
	11.PM	
	12.AM	

BREAKFAST

LUNCH

DINNER

WATER

HAPPY SCALE

MY REWARD

DAILY PLANNER

TODAY IS /

WEATHER

TODAY I AM EXCITED ABOUT

TODAY I AM GRATEFUL FOR

TODAY'S TOP PRIORITY

1.

2.

3.

TO DO LIST

TODAY'S SCHEDULE

PLAN		TRACK
	5.AM	
	6.AM	
	7.AM	
	8.AM	
	9.AM	
	10.AM	
	11.AM	
	12.PM	
	1.PM	
	3.PM	
	4.PM	
	5.PM	
	6.PM	
	7.PM	
	8.PM	
	9.PM	
	10.PM	
	11.PM	
	12.AM	

BREAKFAST

LUNCH

DINNER

WATER

HAPPY SCALE

MY REWARD

DAILY PLANNER

TODAY IS /

WEATHER

TODAY I AM EXCITED ABOUT

TODAY I AM GRATEFUL FOR

TODAY'S TOP PRIORITY

1.

2.

3.

TO DO LIST

TODAY'S SCHEDULE

PLAN		TRACK
	5.AM	
	6.AM	
	7.AM	
	8.AM	
	9.AM	
	10.AM	
	11.AM	
	12.PM	
	1.PM	
	3.PM	
	4.PM	
	5.PM	
	6.PM	
	7.PM	
	8.PM	
	9.PM	
	10.PM	
	11.PM	
	12.AM	

BREAKFAST

LUNCH

DINNER

WATER

HAPPY SCALE

MY REWARD

DAILY PLANNER

TODAY IS /

WEATHER

TODAY I AM EXCITED ABOUT

TODAY I AM GRATEFUL FOR

TODAY'S TOP PRIORITY

1.

2.

3.

TO DO LIST

TODAY'S SCHEDULE

PLAN		TRACK
	5.AM	
	6.AM	
	7.AM	
	8.AM	
	9.AM	
	10.AM	
	11.AM	
	12.PM	
	1.PM	
	3.PM	
	4.PM	
	5.PM	
	6.PM	
	7.PM	
	8.PM	
	9.PM	
	10.PM	
	11.PM	
	12.AM	

BREAKFAST

LUNCH

DINNER

WATER

HAPPY SCALE

MY REWARD

DAILY PLANNER

TODAY IS /

WEATHER

TODAY I AM EXCITED ABOUT

TODAY I AM GRATEFUL FOR

TODAY'S TOP PRIORITY

1.

2.

3.

TO DO LIST

TODAY'S SCHEDULE

PLAN		TRACK
	5.AM	
	6.AM	
	7.AM	
	8.AM	
	9.AM	
	10.AM	
	11.AM	
	12.PM	
	1.PM	
	3.PM	
	4.PM	
	5.PM	
	6.PM	
	7.PM	
	8.PM	
	9.PM	
	10.PM	
	11.PM	
	12.AM	

BREAKFAST

LUNCH

DINNER

WATER

HAPPY SCALE

MY REWARD

DAILY PLANNER

TODAY IS /

WEATHER

TODAY I AM EXCITED ABOUT

TODAY I AM GRATEFUL FOR

TODAY'S TOP PRIORITY

1.

2.

3.

TO DO LIST

TODAY'S SCHEDULE

PLAN		TRACK
	5.AM	
	6.AM	
	7.AM	
	8.AM	
	9.AM	
	10.AM	
	11.AM	
	12.PM	
	1.PM	
	3.PM	
	4.PM	
	5.PM	
	6.PM	
	7.PM	
	8.PM	
	9.PM	
	10.PM	
	11.PM	
	12.AM	

BREAKFAST

LUNCH

DINNER

WATER

HAPPY SCALE

MY REWARD

DAILY PLANNER

TODAY IS /

WEATHER

TODAY I AM EXCITED ABOUT

TODAY I AM GRATEFUL FOR

TODAY'S TOP PRIORITY

1.

2.

3.

TO DO LIST

TODAY'S SCHEDULE

PLAN		TRACK
	5.AM	
	6.AM	
	7.AM	
	8.AM	
	9.AM	
	10.AM	
	11.AM	
	12.PM	
	1.PM	
	3.PM	
	4.PM	
	5.PM	
	6.PM	
	7.PM	
	8.PM	
	9.PM	
	10.PM	
	11.PM	
	12.AM	

BREAKFAST

LUNCH

DINNER

WATER

HAPPY SCALE

MY REWARD

DAILY PLANNER

TODAY IS /

WEATHER

TODAY I AM EXCITED ABOUT

TODAY I AM GRATEFUL FOR

TODAY'S TOP PRIORITY

1.

2.

3.

TO DO LIST

TODAY'S SCHEDULE

PLAN		TRACK
	5.AM	
	6.AM	
	7.AM	
	8.AM	
	9.AM	
	10.AM	
	11.AM	
	12.PM	
	1.PM	
	3.PM	
	4.PM	
	5.PM	
	6.PM	
	7.PM	
	8.PM	
	9.PM	
	10.PM	
	11.PM	
	12.AM	

BREAKFAST

LUNCH

DINNER

WATER

HAPPY SCALE

MY REWARD

DAILY PLANNER

TODAY IS /

WEATHER

TODAY I AM EXCITED ABOUT

TODAY I AM GRATEFUL FOR

TODAY'S TOP PRIORITY

1.

2.

3.

TO DO LIST

TODAY'S SCHEDULE

PLAN		TRACK
	5.AM	
	6.AM	
	7.AM	
	8.AM	
	9.AM	
	10.AM	
	11.AM	
	12.PM	
	1.PM	
	3.PM	
	4.PM	
	5.PM	
	6.PM	
	7.PM	
	8.PM	
	9.PM	
	10.PM	
	11.PM	
	12.AM	

BREAKFAST

LUNCH

DINNER

WATER

HAPPY SCALE

MY REWARD

DAILY PLANNER

TODAY IS /

WEATHER

TODAY I AM EXCITED ABOUT

TODAY I AM GRATEFUL FOR

TODAY'S TOP PRIORITY

1.

2.

3.

TO DO LIST

TODAY'S SCHEDULE

PLAN		TRACK
	5.AM	
	6.AM	
	7.AM	
	8.AM	
	9.AM	
	10.AM	
	11.AM	
	12.PM	
	1.PM	
	3.PM	
	4.PM	
	5.PM	
	6.PM	
	7.PM	
	8.PM	
	9.PM	
	10.PM	
	11.PM	
	12.AM	

BREAKFAST

LUNCH

DINNER

WATER

HAPPY SCALE

MY REWARD

DAILY PLANNER

TODAY IS /

WEATHER

TODAY I AM EXCITED ABOUT

TODAY I AM GRATEFUL FOR

TODAY'S TOP PRIORITY

1.

2.

3.

TO DO LIST

TODAY'S SCHEDULE

PLAN		TRACK
	5.AM	
	6.AM	
	7.AM	
	8.AM	
	9.AM	
	10.AM	
	11.AM	
	12.PM	
	1.PM	
	3.PM	
	4.PM	
	5.PM	
	6.PM	
	7.PM	
	8.PM	
	9.PM	
	10.PM	
	11.PM	
	12.AM	

BREAKFAST

LUNCH

DINNER

WATER

HAPPY SCALE

MY REWARD

DAILY PLANNER

TODAY IS /

WEATHER

TODAY I AM EXCITED ABOUT

TODAY I AM GRATEFUL FOR

TODAY'S TOP PRIORITY

1.

2.

3.

TO DO LIST

TODAY'S SCHEDULE

PLAN		TRACK
	5.AM	
	6.AM	
	7.AM	
	8.AM	
	9.AM	
	10.AM	
	11.AM	
	12.PM	
	1.PM	
	3.PM	
	4.PM	
	5.PM	
	6.PM	
	7.PM	
	8.PM	
	9.PM	
	10.PM	
	11.PM	
	12.AM	

BREAKFAST

LUNCH

DINNER

WATER

HAPPY SCALE

MY REWARD

DAILY PLANNER

TODAY IS /

WEATHER

TODAY I AM EXCITED ABOUT

TODAY I AM GRATEFUL FOR

TODAY'S TOP PRIORITY

1.

2.

3.

TO DO LIST

TODAY'S SCHEDULE

PLAN		TRACK
	5.AM	
	6.AM	
	7.AM	
	8.AM	
	9.AM	
	10.AM	
	11.AM	
	12.PM	
	1.PM	
	3.PM	
	4.PM	
	5.PM	
	6.PM	
	7.PM	
	8.PM	
	9.PM	
	10.PM	
	11.PM	
	12.AM	

BREAKFAST

LUNCH

DINNER

WATER

HAPPY SCALE

MY REWARD

DAILY PLANNER

TODAY IS /

WEATHER

TODAY I AM EXCITED ABOUT

TODAY I AM GRATEFUL FOR

TODAY'S TOP PRIORITY

1.

2.

3.

TO DO LIST

TODAY'S SCHEDULE

PLAN		TRACK
	5.AM	
	6.AM	
	7.AM	
	8.AM	
	9.AM	
	10.AM	
	11.AM	
	12.PM	
	1.PM	
	3.PM	
	4.PM	
	5.PM	
	6.PM	
	7.PM	
	8.PM	
	9.PM	
	10.PM	
	11.PM	
	12.AM	

BREAKFAST

LUNCH

DINNER

WATER

HAPPY SCALE

MY REWARD

DAILY PLANNER

TODAY IS /

WEATHER

TODAY I AM EXCITED ABOUT

TODAY I AM GRATEFUL FOR

TODAY'S TOP PRIORITY

1.

2.

3.

TO DO LIST

TODAY'S SCHEDULE

PLAN		TRACK
	5.AM	
	6.AM	
	7.AM	
	8.AM	
	9.AM	
	10.AM	
	11.AM	
	12.PM	
	1.PM	
	3.PM	
	4.PM	
	5.PM	
	6.PM	
	7.PM	
	8.PM	
	9.PM	
	10.PM	
	11.PM	
	12.AM	

BREAKFAST

LUNCH

DINNER

WATER

HAPPY SCALE

MY REWARD

DAILY PLANNER

TODAY IS /

WEATHER

TODAY I AM EXCITED ABOUT

TODAY I AM GRATEFUL FOR

TODAY'S TOP PRIORITY

1.

2.

3.

TO DO LIST

TODAY'S SCHEDULE

PLAN		TRACK
	5.AM	
	6.AM	
	7.AM	
	8.AM	
	9.AM	
	10.AM	
	11.AM	
	12.PM	
	1.PM	
	3.PM	
	4.PM	
	5.PM	
	6.PM	
	7.PM	
	8.PM	
	9.PM	
	10.PM	
	11.PM	
	12.AM	

BREAKFAST

LUNCH

DINNER

WATER

HAPPY SCALE

MY REWARD

DAILY PLANNER

TODAY IS /

WEATHER

TODAY I AM EXCITED ABOUT

TODAY I AM GRATEFUL FOR

TODAY'S TOP PRIORITY

1.
2.
3.

TO DO LIST

TODAY'S SCHEDULE

PLAN		TRACK
	5.AM	
	6.AM	
	7.AM	
	8.AM	
	9.AM	
	10.AM	
	11.AM	
	12.PM	
	1.PM	
	3.PM	
	4.PM	
	5.PM	
	6.PM	
	7.PM	
	8.PM	
	9.PM	
	10.PM	
	11.PM	
	12.AM	

BREAKFAST

LUNCH

DINNER

WATER

HAPPY SCALE

MY REWARD

DAILY PLANNER

TODAY IS /

WEATHER

TODAY I AM EXCITED ABOUT

TODAY I AM GRATEFUL FOR

TODAY'S TOP PRIORITY

1.
2.
3.

TO DO LIST

TODAY'S SCHEDULE

PLAN		TRACK
	5.AM	
	6.AM	
	7.AM	
	8.AM	
	9.AM	
	10.AM	
	11.AM	
	12.PM	
	1.PM	
	3.PM	
	4.PM	
	5.PM	
	6.PM	
	7.PM	
	8.PM	
	9.PM	
	10.PM	
	11.PM	
	12.AM	

BREAKFAST

LUNCH

DINNER

WATER

HAPPY SCALE

MY REWARD

DAILY PLANNER

TODAY IS /

WEATHER

TODAY I AM EXCITED ABOUT

TODAY I AM GRATEFUL FOR

TODAY'S TOP PRIORITY

1.

2.

3.

TO DO LIST

TODAY'S SCHEDULE

PLAN		TRACK
	5.AM	
	6.AM	
	7.AM	
	8.AM	
	9.AM	
	10.AM	
	11.AM	
	12.PM	
	1.PM	
	3.PM	
	4.PM	
	5.PM	
	6.PM	
	7.PM	
	8.PM	
	9.PM	
	10.PM	
	11.PM	
	12.AM	

BREAKFAST

LUNCH

DINNER

WATER

HAPPY SCALE

MY REWARD

DAILY PLANNER

TODAY IS /

WEATHER

TODAY I AM EXCITED ABOUT

TODAY I AM GRATEFUL FOR

TODAY'S TOP PRIORITY

1.

2.

3.

TO DO LIST

TODAY'S SCHEDULE

PLAN		TRACK
	5.AM	
	6.AM	
	7.AM	
	8.AM	
	9.AM	
	10.AM	
	11.AM	
	12.PM	
	1.PM	
	3.PM	
	4.PM	
	5.PM	
	6.PM	
	7.PM	
	8.PM	
	9.PM	
	10.PM	
	11.PM	
	12.AM	

BREAKFAST

LUNCH

DINNER

WATER

HAPPY SCALE

MY REWARD

DAILY PLANNER

TODAY IS /

WEATHER

TODAY I AM EXCITED ABOUT

TODAY I AM GRATEFUL FOR

TODAY'S TOP PRIORITY

1.

2.

3.

TO DO LIST

TODAY'S SCHEDULE

PLAN		TRACK
	5.AM	
	6.AM	
	7.AM	
	8.AM	
	9.AM	
	10.AM	
	11.AM	
	12.PM	
	1.PM	
	3.PM	
	4.PM	
	5.PM	
	6.PM	
	7.PM	
	8.PM	
	9.PM	
	10.PM	
	11.PM	
	12.AM	

BREAKFAST

LUNCH

DINNER

WATER

HAPPY SCALE

MY REWARD

DAILY PLANNER

TODAY IS /

WEATHER

TODAY I AM EXCITED ABOUT

TODAY I AM GRATEFUL FOR

TODAY'S TOP PRIORITY

1.

2.

3.

TO DO LIST

TODAY'S SCHEDULE

PLAN		TRACK
	5.AM	
	6.AM	
	7.AM	
	8.AM	
	9.AM	
	10.AM	
	11.AM	
	12.PM	
	1.PM	
	3.PM	
	4.PM	
	5.PM	
	6.PM	
	7.PM	
	8.PM	
	9.PM	
	10.PM	
	11.PM	
	12.AM	

BREAKFAST

LUNCH

DINNER

WATER

HAPPY SCALE

MY REWARD

www.ingramcontent.com/pod-product-compliance
Lightning Source LLC
Chambersburg PA
CBHW052341210326
41597CB00037B/6216
9781953638427